MY PEOPLE'S PILGRIMAGE

MY PEOPLE'S
PILGRIMAGE

DIANA GRUFFYDD WILLIAMS

First impression: 2008

© Diana Gruffydd Williams and Y Lolfa Cyf., 2008

This book is subject to copyright
and may not be reproduced by any means
except for review purposes
without the prior written consent of the publishers.

Cover design: Y Lolfa

ISBN: 978-1-84771-043-7

Printed on acid-free and partly recycled paper
and published and bound in Wales by
Y Lolfa Cyf., Talybont, Ceredigion SY24 5AP
e-mail ylolfa@ylolfa.com
website www.ylolfa.com
tel 01970 832 304
fax 832 782

For

Bethan Nia

and

Catrin Elinor

FOREWORD

M Y FATHER DIED IN 2001. When my mother died in November of the following year, she had just managed to see and hold her great-grand-daughter. My grand-daughter has been born into the twenty-first century, yet, through my own personal experiences, I can remember relatives born as early as 1887. If I rely on memories of generations older than myself, the recall naturally reaches back further and, with the additional benefit of census returns, birth, marriage and death certificates, I felt that I had resources that were too valuable to ignore or neglect.

I soon realised that there was more than a personal family history at my disposal. These stories encapsulated the history of a large section of Wales and her people. They cover the rural poverty of the pre-industrial agricultural labourer and the risky lives of those who were involved in the iron and coal industries. They tell of the times before compulsory education, when medicine was unavailable to the poor, when churches and chapels were of paramount importance in spiritual, moral and social life; they also record the fight to keep the old language. Here we see brave, extraordinary people who were usually unimportant in the eyes of the world. Most of them were not even eligible to vote but I have had the privilege of giving them a voice!

In writing these stories, I realise how much social progress we have made in the space of a few generations. Life is a lot easier in so many ways. I began my married life as a mother in a rented house which had no freezer, central heating or washing machine; we had no car. My parents had begun their life together with far less than we had. For my daughter and grand-daughters' generation, life is unimaginable without cars, television, computers, PCs, DVDs, videos, mobile phones, vacuum cleaners, fridges and freezers, washing-machines, tumble dryers, central heating, instant hot water, flush toilets and bathrooms. Medicine has made major strides and I am one of the many millions who would not have survived without its modern advances. However, I feel that we have *lost* a great deal in our frenetic world.

Poverty is unacceptable but our consumer society often leads to restlessness and does not bring lasting happiness. Intelligent and educated people are increasingly deciding to downshift. The slow agricultural techniques with primitive tools created appalling conditions for agricultural labourers two centuries ago but we are now suffering after decades of intensive farming with its use of pesticides and artificial fertilisers. The rapid growth of interest in organic food and the desire to buy locally-produced goods is now attempting to redress that balance.

We live in an increasingly secularised society but there is a great yearning for spirituality. Can we not learn from our ancestors by recognising and respecting their struggles, their values and principles – and salvage some of those strengths? Can we not use them constructively to enrich our own lives?

My People's Pilgrimage is a personal account based on fact, memory, intuition and imagination. It includes a few poems that I have written myself as well as some meditative prayers in the Celtic tradition in Welsh and in English. These use simple language and emphasise the repetitive nature of basic living.

Two poems were written by other people. The first of these, 'Deigryn Galar ar Fedd y Diweddar Martha Lloyd' was penned by Willie Adams – a poet (*bardd gwlad*) from Spittal and the second poem ''NHAD' was written by my late aunt, Nesta Owen.

I have woven all this available material together with documented information about social history and traditional folk customs contemporary to the time.

ACKNOWLEDGEMENTS

I am grateful to all the relatives who have reminisced and helped me to piece together a bigger picture of *My People's Pilgrimage*. I am especially grateful to my husband, Peter, for his computer expertise and his patience in accompanying me in visits to relatives and cemeteries!

I would like to thank Carolyn Jacob, Librarian at the Reference Room (Central Library, Merthyr Tydfil), for being so ready to share her extensive knowledge. I am indebted to the National History Museum at St. Fagan's, Cyfarthfa Castle Museum and the Cynon Valley Museum, Aberdare – for being there. I am grateful to Aberdare Library –and, in particular, to Nick Kelland (Information Services Librarian) for allowing me to use the old photograph of Bute Street (Aberdare). The old photograph of Fishguard Square comes from the Reflective Images series (Port Talbot). I am especially grateful to St. Fagan's for allowing me to use the words of the Harvest chant from Trefor M. Owen's book, *Welsh Folk Customs*.

I am indebted to all the authors of the books/booklets listed in the Bibliography who have helped me extend my knowledge of Wales.

I am profoundly grateful to Richard Davies of Little Newcastle for his constructive comments and his encyclopaedic knowledge of North Pembrokeshire and the Lloyd family, which have been an invaluable source of help. Thanks also go to Nia Williams (for her advice on the Welsh Language), Mrs. Brenda Evans, Jac (Pontiago) Williams, Timothy Derrick (for his knowledge of the Lewis family), Nesta Owen (deceased), Olga Griffiths, Peter George of Llanferran Farm (owner of Bwchdu), Eileen Evans, Peggy Sloman, The Cynon Valley History Society (especially the individual members to whom I've spoken), Rowland Parry (compiler of Abercynon: Past and Present) for his help and courtesy, the Fishguard Tourist Office, the Research Department of the County Library in Haverfordwest, Phoebe Ann Miles (deceased), Jan Tucker, Colin Phillips, Mair Parker, Lawrence George, Graham Griffiths, Elsmor Lewis and Dorothy Horton. I am also indebted to Lefi Gruffudd of Y Lolfa for his encouragement and to my editor, Dafydd Saer, for the necessary 'background' work'.

The refrain used for the sprinkling of the water on New Year's Day was given to me by Richard Davies of Little Newcastle.

DATA

Henry Griffiths was always known as Harry. He was Uncle Harry to many and he was Daddy to his five children. He was my grandfather and I called him Data.

Data and me. Aberdare, 1946.

*I*T WAS 1944. WOUNDED *soldiers filled the wards of the hospital in Aberdare when my mother went into labour. The mid-wife arrived at the last minute but, fortunately, I was born safely in Data's house anyhow. The unattended birth, the worry of a husband serving abroad in the Royal Engineers and a congenital spinal defect took its toll on my mother — and things were made worse when she contracted milk-fever which nearly killed her. Because of her problems, it was often Data who nursed me in the early months. He wrapped me up in a blanket in the traditional Welsh way so that I was carried around with him everywhere, close enough to hear the steady rhythm of his heart-beat. Sometimes, during the day, he took me a mile or so down the valley to see my paternal grandparents. When we were ready to leave, he showed me the moon then tucked me up into the blanket again so that I lay, cocooned like a papoose, as he walked back up the hill until we reached home. Then he lifted my head out of the blanket to show me the moon and the stars again before I settled back into the comfort of the blanket as he opened the door.*

When I was eighteen months old, my father was demobbed. It was the first time that we had seen each other so he was a total stranger. My mother and father had been married for over three years but had spent little time together because of the War. They were passionate people, very much in love, and needed to talk and have a belated honeymoon. Plans needed to be made for the future too; Aberdare and the other towns in the Valleys were very depressed economically. My father had been stationed in Essex and a local woman with influence had told him that she would help him out if he wanted to move to the area with all its prospects once peace was restored.

As all these discussions were taking place, I clung onto the security that was Data. He was nursing me on one of his big chairs at home when my mother came into the room to break the news. She told him that the three of us (my parents and myself) were all going to move up to Essex. Still holding me, he broke down. "Do whatever you like to me!" he wept "but please don't take this child away from me!"

Plans had already been made and a job was waiting for my father. I was just two years of age when I got on the train that took us to Essex. I don't know how much a child of that age can pick up and sense before verbal skills are developed. All that I did know was that my beloved Data wasn't with us. A light went out of my life.

We returned to Aberdare in the school holidays so I had further opportunities to see Data but, strangely enough, I can remember very little about them. I think that I had been so wounded by the separation that I dared not trust in what seemed like the promise of reunion. Christmases – I can recall some of those. There was the excitement of my stocking with its tangerine, nuts and a little toy. And, yes, Santa really had eaten the kipper that I had left for him by the fire. The milk had gone too and I was so glad that he had chosen to eat and drink with me – he must have had a lot of offers! He had even written to thank me for it all – a gift more memorable than the presents themselves! Another Christmas, I had a doll's house. It was very grand and I couldn't believe that I had been so lucky. The front part opened and closed with a little catch so that I could see inside into every room with its home-made furniture and a couple of tiny dolls to use in it.

Food was still being rationed and I was intrigued, one day, as I watched Data cooking some scraps in a saucepan in the kitchen. He stirred them all together and dropped a little bit of hot, left-over fat into the mixture until everything was all brown. Then he spooned it all out carefully so that nothing was left in the pan and rolled it into a ball. As the fat went hard, it turned a dirty white colour and seemed to keep the food in its shape but there were little gaps between the hard fat and the food – like cracked earth when there has been no rain. The ball looked a bit like a faggot and I hoped that it was not going to be our tea. I didn't need to worry – it was for the hungry birds! I went outside with Data as he tied a bit of string to the ball and hung it on the line.

I noticed the picture of a rosy-cheeked cherub with curly hair on the wall. It was the kind of thing that was so popular in Victorian times and, at my request, I was lifted up to see it better. I wanted to know if it was me! It obviously wasn't me but I couldn't bear the thought of another

13

child being on Data's wall so I persisted until everyone agreed that, yes, it was me! That made me very happy when I went to bed because I knew that wherever I was, even if I was back in Essex, I was always on the wall in Data's big kitchen too. These were small, insignificant recollections for something that was so important to me.

Sometimes, Data came to visit or stay with us in Essex. He had a job as an Insurance Collector for the Hearts of Oak Benefit Society so it was fairly easy for him to change his base for short periods without losing his job. When he was with us, his patch was in the East End of London and, if he was working at the weekends, he took me up with him. I've never met a person who could make everything seem so interesting! Stories, stories, everywhere and Data would even tell me tales about the people we were going to visit.

As we approached one house, he said, "Now, these people are very nice but they don't wash up very well. If they offer us a cup of tea and you're thirsty, take the cup but hold it in your left hand and drink from that side. There won't be any germs!"

Data knocked at the door and spoke to the man in a Cockney accent. He told me that it made people feel more at ease if you talked like them. Wonderfully, Data became a Londoner as he said, "Good morning, guv!"

We must have looked an unlikely couple – the big expansive moustached Welshman with a trilby and a little girl with a seersucker dress and puffed sleeves.

"Good morning, Mr. Griffiths. Come in! Is this your little grand-daughter?"

I nodded shyly as I looked around the room to see if there were any germs or dirty cups.

The man went to get his Hearts of Oak Benefit Society book and said, "Would you like a cup of tea, Mr. Griffiths – and what about your little grand-daughter?"

Data said that he'd love a cup of tea and I nodded shyly. I smiled and watched as we were each handed a china cup full of steaming tea that rested on its floral saucer. Could you see germs, I wondered? What did they look like? I wasn't sure but, glancing across at Data, who winked at me, I turned the cup round and drank using my left hand. Everything would be alright and this was a very exciting adventure!

And so it went on. We'd go to the open markets where Data would always bargain for everything – china, fruit, vegetables, clothes. The Cockney accent came out again as he tried his luck.

"What d'you want for this, guv?"

"For you, I'll do it for a shilling!"

"It's not worth a shilling. Ninepence!"

"I'll be robbing myself for just ninepence!"

"Ninepence ha'penny!"

"Pity my poor wife and children if I give it to you for such a price!"

Data looked in his trousers' pocket and found ninepence. "I don't seem to have the ha'penny," he protested as he handed over the money. The goods were wrapped in newspaper and off we'd go for the next adventure! It was all a game and I knew from the smile on the sellers' faces that their wives and children would be alright.

If Data wasn't working at the weekends, he'd take me to the sea to breathe in the ozone that was supposed to be good for my chronic catarrh. He'd pick up stones and each stone had a story. Shells were held to our ears so that we could hear the tides of the sea cascading into our lives. I never really heard it myself but I wanted to so much that I made myself believe it. We got on a boat that went from Tilbury to a foreign land called Kent. The Kentish town we docked at was called Gravesend, which didn't sound a very happy place but we had a lot of fun there with bits of wood and shops and walks. It was very flat in Kent – a bit like Essex.

And, when these days were over and I was tired, Data and I climbed onto a Primrose coach at Bow. I cuddled up to his warm, sturdy body and he told me stories of adventurers and travellers, stowaways and gypsies!

It was wonderful!

Data was a charmer and I was not the only one to fall under his spell. The local doctor in our Essex village was one of its most respected inhabitants. He practised from home with one of his rooms used as a surgery and another as a pharmacy. His wife, Mildred, was an attractive woman with a strong personality who was always around acting as a comforter, receptionist or bottle-of-medicine labeller. In those days when the status of the doctor and his wife was so very high, Mildred expected the respect that she usually received. However, there were occasions when male patients or visitors tried to be flirtatious and her immediate response was to slap their faces. Data took Mildred a stone that he'd found, saying that he wanted her to have it because it was the same colour as her eyes. Mildred blushed like a young girl and received it with great pleasure. She was smitten.

My parents had worked hard and saved so that they could buy a new, semi-detached house. One day, not long after our prestigious move, Data and I were in the ironmonger's shop in our little village and he and the owner began 'talking trade'.

"These little birds I've got," the man said, as he pointed to a stack of small brown boxes with pierced holes on the top, "these little birds are going to catch on in a big way". Data became the businessman with the Cockney accent again as he looked inside the little box that was handed to him. I sidled up to try to get a glimpse of what was causing the constant little chirrups that were disturbing the peace of the otherwise uneventful, musty shop with its mouse-traps, bottles of turpentine, glue and sandpaper. The box was only opened an inch or two and I just about managed to glimpse a little bird with a blue breast. It was so pretty but, before I had time to admire it, the lid was replaced. The chirrups continued. It seemed that these birds were called budgerigars. They were no trouble to keep but they made excellent company – 'especially for your little grand-daughter'. A little bit of seed every day and water – that's all they needed. They were happy little things; a bit of cuttlefish was always appreciated – but this was a luxury and not at all necessary as they managed very well with the seed alone. Oh, and, yes, and he did stock the bird seed, cuttlefish and cages at very reasonable prices. They could stay in their cages all the time without getting distressed but you could let them out for an hour or so, if you wished. We looked at the cages. The man had obviously invested a lot of money in the hope of successfully marketing these little creatures. I had never had a pet! The man struck up a deal with Data and, before I knew it, the bird was mine.

I carried my prize possession home very carefully in its box. What should I call her? For some reason, I decided on the name Bunty. I walked through the door so full of excitement that I could hardly wait to show my parents. They didn't appear to share my enthusiasm. The little bird, poor thing, flew out of its box and nervously settled on the window frame in our brand new, sparkling house. After her long journey, Bunty didn't know what to make of her new premises and generously endowed the polished sill with her droppings. The cage? Oh, yes, we had been so carried away with Bunty and her feed that we had left the cage in the shop. Oh dear! What a welcome for a budgerigar that had seen nothing but four cardboard walls for days!

Late in the night, when it was very dark but still light enough for me to see things as shadows, I crept downstairs to see what had happened to Bunty. Data was asleep on the armchair with his hands sealed together to make a little human nest. Bunty seemed fine and the cage was collected in the morning.

I became ill when Data left after an extended stay with us in Essex. I was twelve years old. I had been right not to trust in the idea that people you love very much will stay with you. (My paternal grandfather had died a year earlier.) I developed an obsessive phobia that focused on the fear of going blind. Whenever I went to bed, I waited until my parents were asleep and then I made a forlorn little journey around the house, quietly switching all the lights on in turn so that I could check that I had not gone blind. I even managed to find a technique of moving the switches so delicately that they made no noise. Once I had tested my vision on the landing, I'd go downstairs and repeat my trials in the rooms downstairs.

Eventually, when I had covered the entire house, I returned to my bedroom – only to start the whole process again. I continued these desperate rituals until I was exhausted. When my parents discovered my secret, they were horrified. At the time, mental illness was an unmentionable, ridiculed disease associated with shame. Psychiatry was still in its infancy and there was very little information or help available. My parents tried initially to talk to me but I was locked up in some dark, abysmal cave beyond reason – and no one held the key. The light was left on in the landing for me but that didn't solve matters. I thought that my vision might be restricted to the area around the landing so I still needed to check the rest of the house. I was given a night-light but that had the same effect. In a final effort to cure the problem, my mother slept with me in the spare bedroom – but that didn't help either. I used to creep out of the bed when she was asleep to test the lights, going on tiptoe so that I wouldn't wake her. She usually did wake up in spite of my efforts and my behaviour was making her restless. We were at the end of the road. Nothing worked and, now, in addition to my problems, my mother was losing sleep too. I didn't need company, I needed certainty *– and, bleakly, I realised that there were no certainties to be had anywhere. The fact was this; I loved people and then they went away or died. I felt like the ash in the grate when the fire had gone out. No-one seemed to have any idea of how frightened and lonely I was! I decided that I wouldn't worry anymore about going blind – I would just* go *blind. It wouldn't be so bad – and at least I would get some sympathy. As soon as I got to this point, the phobia disappeared. All that happened was that the anxieties shunted themselves back into my unconscious mind – where they remained for many years. But, in the short term, life at home was a lot easier and, to my surprise, I kept my eyesight.*

Data returned to his large Victorian terraced house in Aberdare. He rented a couple of the downstairs rooms to lodgers but, otherwise, he was alone. He had good friends, especially members of the chapel, but, at the end of the day, when he pulled the curtains and checked the fire, this gregarious man who had always been surrounded by people, was lonely.

His sister, Phoebe, was about to retire after a lifetime in service and she had nowhere to live. This helped him make the decision to leave Aberdare and return to Goodwick in his native Pembrokeshire to make a home for her and himself. He chose another large three-storey house on the main street that led down to the sea. Phoebe came to join him there where the kitchen alone was almost as big as the entire cottage where they had spent their childhood. There were three spacious reception rooms on the ground floor and the massive kitchen opened onto a back-garden that was almost vertical. It needed leg muscles that were used to hills to reach – let alone tend. But tend it they did – and it flourished. On the first floor, there were several bedrooms and a bathroom with more bedrooms and another bathroom on the second floor. Data had developed an interest in antique furniture by this time and went to auctions to acquire all sorts of fascinating things. There were monks' chairs, a monk's bench, grandfather clocks and heavy wardrobes filling the rooms with interest and originality.

Who were Henry Griffiths' people?

DAVID and ANNE GRIFFITHS at Mathri

There was no more work for David and Anne Griffiths in Llanhowel in 1848. As agricultural labourers, they relied on the farmers for employment and the farmers themselves were dependent on the mixed fortunes of their land and the kindness or cruelty of the weather. The couple were no strangers to change as Anne had already moved from Llandissilio and David was born in Hayscastle. These were small villages in the heart of rural Pembrokeshire so they had never travelled far – and their new home was only another short journey away. They prepared to move yet again.

David and Anne and their young family were good, reliable workers so, when the annual leasing of labourers was made at the local Fair, they were accepted by a farmer from the nearby village of Mathri. They were able to borrow a horse and cart for the day that was big enough to take their few items of furniture. David hauled the big items onto the cart and tied the pots and pans in an old corn sack. Little Benjamin was given charge of that – so he managed to climb onto the cart and get a free ride! David didn't look back as he led the horse. There was no point in having regrets and sighing for what was gone. Anne walked behind her husband. As a woman, she was not allowed to deal with horses and, anyway, her youngest son, John, wanted to be carried. The couple were middle-aged (they were both born in 1812) and their oldest children had already left home.

They didn't speak much on the journey but their pace quickened as they began to climb the hill to Mathri and they finally exchanged a smile. Here it was – their new cottage! Benjamin and John, pleased to have arrived, went inside to look. David and Anne didn't take long to arrange the furniture which they placed in the middle of the room downstairs to make a partition. Planks had been set above part of the lower room to make a loft and this was where they would all sleep. Benjamin took the roughly-woven coverlets up for their beds. There was no time to waste so David lit the fire and, once it had taken, it would never be allowed to go out again. It was needed every day − even in the summer. Anne went to fetch some water which she brought back and poured into the cauldron that was hooked up above the fire. Every drop of water that came from the well and the stream was so precious!

She found David outside. He'd already dug into the earth and, lifting a clump of soil into his hands, he smiled. When he saw Anne coming to join him, he handed her the same soil to feel and smell. This was the earth from the little patch where they'd be allowed to grow their own vegetables. She smiled nervously. Yes, the earth seemed rich enough!

Anne walked away alone and stared down at the countryside below. Would their move to Mathri be a good one? She looked up at the sky. They needed more than a patch of rich soil. They needed the sun − but not enough to crack the dry earth open. They needed rain − but not so much that it rotted the roots. There were four mouths to feed − and the pig! Anne shivered and drew her shawl around her even though she was not cold. Soon, there would be another little one to feed for she knew that there was a new baby growing inside her.

Mathri stood proudly on its high ground that had been inhabited for centuries. People said that the settlement went back to the Iron Age and the cromlech close by was supposed to be 5000 years old. Five thousand years! Anne reckoned that all this history was a good sign of fertile ground. The Fair and Market were certainly flourishing and crowds came from miles around to trade − so surely it would all turn out well for the Griffiths family. So many of their neighbours had left the countryside altogether for new industries in the South. Others had taken the boat to America. Casting a final glance at the land around her, Anne hoped and prayed that they would not be forced to do the same. They were country people; they *belonged* to Pembrokeshire.

David began work immediately and, as a labourer, he just followed the farmer's instructions. Most of his time was spent in the fields but there were the animals to tend as well. The day began early. As soon as the dawning sun streaked a glimmer of light into the darkness of their little cottage, he knew it was time to start work – and he would only finish his duties when the light began to fade in the evening. Thankfully, there were a few breaks during the day when food was brought out to all the men in the fields. A hunk of bread and cheese and a cup of tea were always so welcomed! Sometimes, there was buttermilk too and oatmeal but it was *cawl* that David looked forward to more than anything else. What better treat could anyone want than that warm, tasty broth with lamb and vegetables?

Anne had to work as well, helping to prepare the food in the farmhouse, churning the butter and baking the oatcakes. Even little Benjamin and John could pick up stones from the field and do some weeding. They had been shown how to tell the difference between the grasses that gave them food and the ones that crept in, quickly and dangerously, to rob them of it.

Anne had her baby – another son, Owen, and, carrying him in her shawl, she continued working, stopping only to give him the breast.

In exchange for all their labour, David and Anne received little financial reward. Not a lot of money changed hands and, even after a session of very heavy work, they usually received an extra payment in kind – some milk, perhaps, a bag of corn or a sack of manure. Complaining was not their right and, of course, they were only able to stay in their cottage as long as there remained work for them to do.

In the summer, the long days made the workload heavier but this was all worthwhile if the crops were successful. They sweated through the hay-making but, when it was finished, there was so much joy – and everyone shared in the wonderful harvest supper. This was the season when the family returned home exhausted, fit for nothing but bed.

The winter was another matter. The days were short and there was less to do on the farm. After a good potato broth with onion in the evening, the family was usually together for several hours before bed-time so they needed something to keep them busy. This was the time for knitting or spinning the hemp that the men had collected earlier in the year – and it was also a time for singing and telling stories by rush-light.

BENJAMIN GRIFFITHS at Mathri

Young Benjamin was always keen to help the grown-ups pick the rushes in the summer and place them out to dry in the sunshine. When they had hardened, he watched as his father, David, made the candles themselves. The dry rush was quickly dipped into hot tallow once or twice and then lifted out quickly with its new coating of bacon or mutton fat and placed onto a slate slab to dry. The children couldn't wait for the time when they'd be able to do all this themselves! There was always the glow from the fire but it was mainly the rush-lights that helped them see what they were doing. They burned down quickly so Benjamin enjoyed the task of turning them at different angles to keep them going a bit longer.

Sometimes, neighbours from another cottage came to join them for the evening. All the men and women who knitted stockings were so used to it that they didn't even need to concentrate on the stitches. The children watched carefully and, as soon as their fingers could manage it, they were knitting too. Stockings could sell for a few pennies in Mathri Fair – a useful income in those lean and chilly months.

The evening's work was well under way when the singing and story-telling began. Nobody had been to school so they only knew what they had been taught in church or chapel. However, though few of the adults could read or write, they knew long lines of poetry by heart and all the verses of the old folk songs. It was wonderful to hear it all and Benjamin was the first to clap even if he didn't always understand everything. On nights such as these, everybody laughed and forgot about the cold winds that were blowing under the doors.

After the singing, was someone about to tell a story? Yes! Benjamin was very happy and listened hard to every word so that he could remember the tales and tell them himself later on. There were so many of them that he could scarcely take them all in! Some came from the *Mabinogion* and others were as old as the hills. Lots of things had happened in Mathri itself and, although the account of the plague of locusts two hundred years back was a good one, the best story for Benjamin was the one about the Martyrs that gave Mathri its name.

Another rush-candle was lit as Benjamin sat on the floor with his little brothers. Their eyes were sore from the burning tallow but they were in the best place, away from the worst of the smelly smoke! Their friend and neighbour – another farm-hand, began slowly in his native Welsh.

"One day, long ago," he said seriously, "there was a woman here in Pembrokeshire – yes, here in our own part of the world!" He was enjoying himself as he leant forward to give the tale some extra excitement. He stopped for a moment to get everyone's attention, then whispered, "She gave birth to seven sons all on the same day! Yes, indeed, seven sons on one day!" Everyone looked surprised even though they knew what was coming next. "Well, her husband was *not* pleased. How would he be able to feed seven sons?" Everyone shook their heads solemnly at the question. "Aha!" Benjamin smiled – this was great fun! "Well!"

Again the friend paused. "Well, the husband decided that he would *drown* the seven boys!" Everyone looked horrified! "Yes, he decided to drown them! And, when he had finished his evil deed and left them in the river, St. Teilo appeared! Yes, St. Teilo himself!"

Thank goodness the good saint had turned up, thought Benjamin. The rush-light had almost burnt down again but everyone wanted to wait and hear the end of the story. It seemed that the Saint had rescued the boys and promised to give them a Christian upbringing. Teilo brought them to Mathri and they were well-fed because a fish appeared miraculously every day on the water's edge for them to eat. And, when their life's journey was over, they became the Mathri Martyrs who were buried right beside them in the churchyard.

There were smiles all round as the story ended and, when Benjamin thought about the old burial chambers, the Iron Age settlement, the cromlech at Carreg Samson, the round churchyard wall that had been there before Jesus Christ was born, it was very easy to believe the story, yes, every word of it!

Benjamin was born in Llanhowel in 1844 and worked in Mathri as a very young lad. It was only little tasks at first but, as time went by, he was sharing the same hard working hours as his father. By the time he was twelve, he was doing a man's job as an agricultural labourer. This was very helpful for David and Anne, who needed the extra shilling or two. All the farming was done by hand and it took strong muscles and patience to work the land with the scythe, the weeding-hook or the pitchfork for hours on end. They all spent half their lives with their backs bent over and Benjamin's hands had already hardened from the constant pressure. He was a man!

At busy times of the farming year, everyone, including the labourers, co-operated to get the work done. Hay-making needed to be done quickly and the only way to complete it was to use every pair of hands for miles around. The farmers made arrangements so that hay-making was done on different days on each farm. And so it was that Benjamin, along with his brothers and parents, travelled across the villages of North Pembrokeshire to help out whenever and wherever they were needed – in Manorowen, Trefasser, St. Nicholas, Llanwnda… Unless it had been a bad year for the crops, everyone looked forward to these occasions. They were hard work but gave everyone an opportunity to meet up with old friends and relatives, laugh and share a meal together. What greater joy could there be than to work together in the fields and see something achieved – a field with its hay made in the sunshine or a harvest safely gathered in?

Benjamin had known Margaret Jenkins since childhood. Her father was another agricultural labourer and the family lived in Gwndwngwyn cottage near Trefasser. They all met up at these busy times of the year but, once they were growing out of childhood, they began to notice each other in a different kind of way. It all began with a smile – and a smile can say many things! Wearing his flat cap, clogs and woollen clothes in the heat of the summer, Benjamin was exhausted by mid-day and more than ready for the cup of tea and buttermilk that the women brought out for all the men in the fields. He was very pleased if it was Margaret who handed him the cup. But, as the romance began to blossom, would Margaret make a suitable wife for Benjamin?

THOMAS and PHOEBE JENKINS
at Gwndwngwyn

Margaret Jenkins' childhood home, Gwndwngwyn, stood defiantly on an isolated hill that faced the wild sea at Pwllderi on the south-western coast of the Pencaer Peninsular. This was the home of her parents, Thomas and Phoebe Jenkins but, earlier, Thomas had lived there with his first wife, Martha.

Thomas Jenkins was born in 1804 on this rugged patch of land and he learnt about the seasons, the soil and the sea as soon as he could dress himself. Young Thomas would never know anything but the harshness of the agricultural labourer's plight. This land with its thinner soil was pitted with stones and not as fertile as that in Mathri – but Thomas had been working on it from the age of six and he understood it well. Without any other experience of life to make comparisons, Thomas accepted the long working-hours, poor rewards and meagre food rations in exchange for the right to live in his tied cottage and grow vegetables on the farmer's land.

However difficult things were, Thomas grew up proud of an event that had happened just seven years before his birth in 1797. It had brought all the local people of every status close together and it was still the talk of the summer gatherings and the long winter evenings. Thomas' own people had helped to defeat an invading French army! How could any of them forget such a thing?

A man near St. David's had been the first to notice three French ships at sea with troops on board. He set off on horseback to tell the local people and they all watched with alarm. Then, it happened – the French actually landed on Welsh soil with their arms! The crowd from St. David's made their way towards craggy Carregwastad Point, near Llanwnda, calling on all able-bodied men to join them as they went. Even farm labourers were urged to leave the fields to swell their numbers because nothing was more important than defending the land. Some of the Welsh men had guns and pistols – others just straightened their scythes and fixed them on long poles. They carried on their way, gathering more men all the time as they reached every new village or hamlet. Even so – for all their efforts, the Welshmen were greatly outnumbered when they finally arrived but the invaders were mistaken if they thought they were going to win this territory easily. Thomas' own relatives were there and he was so proud of them.

When Thomas grew to be a man, he married a local girl, Martha, and the couple went to live at Gwndwngwyn, where Martha had their three children. From their work with the animals, farm-labourers knew more than anyone the tremendous risks there were in producing livestock – and there were similar dangers for their own women. A man hoped for a wife who would bear him many children – the extra mouths to feed were soon out earning a small wage. The boys took their turn in the fields and the girls helped out as farm servants. But pregnancy brought its own problems. Many women died of infections or excessive bleeding and babies failed to thrive in the womb. Even after a safe delivery, there was the worry of the dreaded 'milk fever' and further illnesses. Martha was one of those women who lost the fight. She died. So many families had suffered similar losses and there was a close and loving bond between all the local people in the community. Everybody helped Thomas and the children and no-one could have wanted more support. They all came into the cottage – one to lay Martha out in the open coffin at home, someone else to tidy the house and take care of the children; friends and relatives came with food for the funeral feast. A collection was made so that the Minister could have his fee for a proper funeral. Martha was laid to rest.

Thomas was a widower with three children who had to continue working if he wanted to keep his home. The oldest boy was nine and already earning a few pennies but the two younger children weren't ready to help him in the fields yet. They needed a mother. Phoebe Davies from Fishguard was working in Llanwnda as a farm servant at the time and was already well-known by the family. Thomas and Phoebe married and the new bride was taken to live at Gwndwngwyn. There, Phoebe took her step-children under her wing and produced six more children with Thomas. Fortunately, she was a strong woman and survived all the demands on her body, giving birth to her youngest child when she was 46 years old.

Their simple life at Gwndwngwyn was greatly influenced by the sea as they were just a few fields away from the crags and ferns that led down sharply to the shore. The sound of the crashing waves was always present and, although they had fine views right over to St. David's, the family saw the havoc the sea caused for the boats that were bold enough to venture there in rough weather. Thomas and Phoebe had witnessed frequent shipwrecks. People living in this tough place had always seen that same sea, relentless when it chose to be, as if pleased by its own savagery. Then it would turn, like a fickle animal, to shimmer and expose its clear, blue glory. In the olden times, there had been others who had seen the antics of the seals that came up to bask on the beach below, waiting to give birth to their young. From the summit of nearby Garn Fawr, the highest hill in the area, an Iron Age fort and ancient burial chambers could be seen. Yes, people had been here since the beginning of time!

The beauty and history of their home setting didn't help them to live, of course, and Thomas continued to work hard, struggling to manage by tending to the crops, the sheep and cattle every day. Phoebe was a good farm servant and earned a few extra pennies by making up herbal medicines for the farmers' wives. Her three oldest children were boys and they were soon out helping their father in the fields but life was so unpredictable and, in 1859, there were terrible gales and storms that caused chaos and devastation right across Pembrokeshire. It took a long time for country people to recover from the ruthlessness of Nature but, in the following year, Phoebe had Margaret – the first of her three daughters. A new year had come with a new child and she gave them hope for the future. Margaret was soon taking her turn in helping out at home and looking after her two little sisters.

The whole family turned out for the potato lifting. It was cheaper to employ women and children for this tedious work so Phoebe and her daughters were kept busy. The constant bending made their backs ache but they had to keep going. Phoebe or Margaret stopped from time to time to attend to the little ones and sometimes it was hard to be cheerful – bending, picking, throwing the potatoes into a basket all day with the sun on their backs. At least they weren't living in Ireland, where the potatoes had been ruined by blight. Yes, Thomas and Phoebe and their family had to thank God for the healthy vegetables they were lifting from the Pembrokeshire soil.

At the end of days like this, they were exhausted when they made the return journey to Gwndwngwyn, and Thomas told the story of the French invasion again to amuse his weary children.

"The French Army was twice the size of ours," he said loudly, trying to keep them awake until they arrived home. "We let them land at Carregwastad and they broke into our houses. They set up their headquarters at Trehowel Farm where *we* help at harvest-time. There had been a shipwreck, you see, and there was plenty of wine and good food at Trehowel. It's funny how things turn out! The French ate too much, got drunk and lost their senses. After that, it was easy…"

Phoebe smiled at Thomas. She was carrying one of her little daughters and Margaret was carrying the baby. They had fallen asleep in spite of the tale.

All the children were glad to go straight up to the loft to lie close together in the beds they shared. Phoebe looked at the butter they had been given as wages for their day's work and placed it downstairs in the little area she used as a dairy. Thomas heaved the bag of grain he'd been given onto his shoulders to store it up in the loft so that mice and rats wouldn't rob them of their precious food.

It was late and Thomas and Phoebe only had to tend to the

fire. Almost too tired to talk, Phoebe muttered, "Funny about old Enoch's dream, wasn't it?"

"Aye!" Thomas smiled. Phoebe loved recounting this tale – something to do with women's intuitions, he supposed. Enoch Lale, a local man, had dreamt that the French were invading Llanwnda, thirty years before it actually happened. His dream had been so real that he woke his wife and went out in the night to see what was going on. He had heard the French men, who, certain of victory, were banging their brass drums down Goodwick Hill. Poor old Enoch told several people about this dream and everybody laughed. Thirty years later, those who were still alive laughed no more when they saw the dream coming true before their very eyes. Even the details were correct for the invaders banged their drums in the same way!

"Yes, funny about old Enoch's dream!" Thomas agreed.

It was time for bed and there was more potato lifting the next day. The couple said The Lord's Prayer together. He had given them their daily bread.

MARGARET JENKINS at Gwndwngwyn

Margaret Jenkins often took her two little sisters walking but it was not just for pleasure. Once the last spring frost had passed, the family was allowed to cut peat as fuel for their fire and, when *that* had been used, they had to search elsewhere. Thomas let the girls have the wooden barrow he'd made and off they went to collect gorse! It grew everywhere around their home and the more they collected the better. Farmers used it to feed their animals and paid them a couple of pennies for their efforts – but they were able to keep the rest for themselves as fuel. The gorse burned quickly and crackled away, filling the cottage with its smoke – but it was better than nothing and it lasted longer than dried cow-dung. Gorse pulling is harsh on the hands and, though Margaret's hands were already toughened by work, it hurt her little sisters. They sat down for a moment as Margaret rubbed and kissed their hands.

"Tell us about Jemima Nicholas!" the little girls said.

Margaret knew the story well (she had heard it often enough!) but she was happy to tell it again. "Oh, Jemima!" she exclaimed.

"Yes, Jemima!" the little girls cried.

"Well, Jemima knew that all the men were going up to Llanwnda to face the French army," Margaret began, "and she wanted to do something herself! She was a big lady, tough, a cobbler, and set off with a pitchfork in her hand! Lots of other ladies joined her and, when the Frenchmen saw them with their red cloaks and tall black hats and the pitchforks that looked *very* dangerous – and remember that the French men were drunk! Well, they thought there was another band of soldiers coming up to fight them!"

"And they were frightened? Did they really think they were men?"

Margaret looked tenderly at their eager little faces. "Oh, yes, they were frightened!" she replied, smiling. "And, yes, the French *did* think they were men. They all gave themselves up down on Goodwick Sands".

Margaret stood up even as she was finishing the story because there was no time to waste. "Come on!" she chided, softly "Let's get some more gorse!"

The three of them were pleased with themselves as they filled the cart. They would have a good fire tonight!

Story-telling to her sisters came to an end when Margaret was eleven because she left home to become a farm servant in Ffynnondruidion Farm in Llanwnda. It was an ancient and mysterious place with holy wells in its grounds and Margaret was glad of this easily accessible water as she did all her tasks. She wasn't totally separated from her family because Sunday was always a day of rest and they all met up at chapel before sharing a meal together. They soon realised that Margaret had something – or someone – on her mind. It was Benjamin Griffiths from Mathri!

It was a long courtship as there were few opportunities to meet – and times were so hard. Margaret's father, Thomas, died and her mother, Phoebe, was left in a miserable situation. She had no money, couldn't stay on at Gwndwngwyn as a widow and, at the age of 60, she was nothing more than a homeless pauper. Although this meant the Workhouse for some, Phoebe's unmarried sister came to the rescue. She was working as a char maid in Llanwnda and the two women shared the same cottage. All Phoebe's children, including Margaret, helped their mother with a few shillings here and there, half a sack of potatoes or a small bag of grain. A wedding had to wait!

Benjamin and Margaret were eventually married on an October day in 1875. The harvest had been safely gathered in and Phoebe was more settled when the bride, given away by her oldest brother, was finally able to marry. The couple had never been to school, of course, but a lot had been learnt at Sunday School and Benjamin was proud to be able to sign his name on the wedding certificate. Margaret hadn't learnt how to write so she was shown where to sign with a cross. They were man and wife!

What would become of this younger generation of agricultural labourers who were about to start life together?

BENJAMIN and MARGARET GRIFFITHS
at Bwchdu and Castell

Benjamin and Margaret walked to their new home. The cottage, Bwchdu, was even more isolated than their childhood homes, in the middle of nowhere in particular, north of Mathri, south of Llanwnda – and very close to the sea. It was owned by the farmer at Llanferran who let them live there, grow their own vegetables in a small enclosed garden and keep some pigs and cattle in exchange for their labour.

As Benjamin and Margaret approached the cottage, they saw the little garden, the pig-sty and cattle-shed before they took a look inside. The single room downstairs had an earthen floor and was partitioned by furniture to form two rooms. The smaller section was being used as a bedroom at night; there was already another couple living in Bwchdu with their young children – the cottage was to be shared. The other family welcomed them and showed them in to the larger area downstairs where they stopped to talk for a moment. This was the hub of the home with its *simne fawr* (the big chimney) and the constant fire over which some *cawl* was being cooked. Oatcakes were being made in front of the fire, some butter had been churned and the pig, that had just been killed and bled, was hanging up, salted. The two families looked up at it gratefully for this would be their source of meat during the winter.

They all climbed the little wooden ladder to look at the straw beds in the half-loft. One day, their own children would sleep up there but, before anything else, Benjamin and Margaret needed to settle in and begin work. The hours were long but that was nothing new to either of them.

Life had always been based on the rhythms of the farming year and the sea around them. Sheep-shearing was a busy time at Bwchdu and Benjamin was returning home one day after he'd taken the fleeces down to the woollen mill nearby. He looked over at the stunning views right over to St. David's Head but his heart was not softened at the beautiful sight. The moods of the sea were familiar to them both. Margaret, especially, knew all its whims – her nose could sense the coming of a storm or a gale in the salty air. It was true that the storms brought their own gifts but it was at the cost of others. Margaret often climbed down the crags to the shore after a rough storm. She found driftwood there to keep the fire going, succulent sea-weed that made a delicious supper when mixed with oatmeal – and, occasionally, there was a crab!

Life in the sea-swept cottage was a constant struggle and Margaret began to have her babies – four of them in as many years. Sarah arrived first in 1877, then, John, Phoebe and David. In those four years, Margaret had been extremely fortunate – the babies were strong and healthy and she had survived herself. But Bwchdu was now very crowded. The other couple had five children so there were thirteen people cramped together. Both women were still of childbearing age so the situation would only get worse.

Benjamin's lease at Bwchdu ended in 1883 when Margaret was expecting yet another baby. Another farmer employed Benjamin and the family walked up the few miles to their new cottage in Llanwnda. Castell was, if anything, smaller than the one they'd left but they had it to themselves. Benjamin began work straightaway in Trehowel Farm and the couple had another son, Thomas. Two years later, little Thomas died – just at the time that Margaret knew that she was expecting the next child. They had seen death many times before, of course, but nothing prepares a parent for a child's loss. He was the little boy she had carried in her womb, nursed at her breast and now he was lifeless in the tiny coffin on the table. There was nothing to be done but look forward to the next baby. Flowers could be placed on the grave on *Sul y Blodau* (Palm Sunday – traditionally a time when the Welsh decorated and attended to the graves) but they had to carry on living. When the next baby arrived, little William seemed healthy enough and, a year later, Margaret gave birth to yet another son, called James. James became ill at the age of two. The only medicine was native wisdom and the herbs of the fields. Margaret put cold compresses in place, waiting for the crisis, hoping and praying that he would live. At the same time, she had to care for her other children who were still very young and, as for Benjamin, if he didn't carry on working, they'd lose the cottage. In spite of everyone's efforts, little James died and, once again, family and friends filled the cottage to offer their sympathy and practical help.

Margaret was carrying another baby when she and Benjamin went up to the farm to look at the new tools that had arrived. They were excited to see how much easier their work would be – but it wasn't long before they grasped the truth of the situation. Whereas a farmer had needed four labourers before, he now only needed one. Their lives had been tough but the land had always offered them some sort of a living. Now, it had finally failed them. Agricultural labourers were desperate and hundreds of people were streaming out of the country-side just to survive. Only big landowners were able to afford the latest tools and equipment so, as they became richer, they bought up even more land from the small farmers who were selling up because they couldn't compete. The new baby – another boy, Henry, arrived in 1887 so there were now eight mouths to feed. Henry, an endearing little child, was known to everyone as Harry, but what future was there for him and his family? The old traditional ways of farming had changed and Benjamin and Margaret faced one of the hardest decisions of their lives.

Benjamin would have to leave Llanwnda and join the men who had gone away for the industries. He had no other choice. Margaret was carrying yet another baby. The couple were middle-aged – past forty. If Benjamin left, he'd have to do what all the other men did. He'd have to find lodgings, share a room with several other men until he'd saved enough money to share with just one other man. The process would go on until he had saved enough money to rent a terraced house. This would take years to achieve and, if he and Margaret survived that long, they would be old. Benjamin decided to go alone and send money home to Margaret so that she could stay in the cottage and feed herself and the children. As soon as he could, he'd return to her and his native Pembrokeshire. Margaret had all her family around her for support; her mother-in-law, Anne, long widowed and a pauper, was living next door with her grand-daughter.

Margaret had never left the wild Pencaer peninsula and Benjamin's experience was not much wider. He left with a heavy heart, walking along the country lanes that he knew so well, down the hill to Goodwick and up into the town of Fishguard, where the horse and cart was waiting at the Square to take him to meet the train. His journey was a lonely one but he had to make it! Would Margaret's health hold? Would he ever see his ageing mother again? What of the new baby? Would the children forget him? For the first time in his life, he would be working *under* the ground, not *on* it! He had the right to vote now so maybe there was a fairer world ahead?

As he travelled, the landscape changed. There were the lush hills of Carmarthenshire and, at first, the Glamorganshire countryside didn't seem too different but then, all of a sudden, he saw things that were almost unbelievable. The hills were darker and there were wheels of coal-mines standing out everywhere against the sky-line. Nothing had prepared him for the valleys themselves. Instead of crags and gorse and sparkling rivers, there were rows and rows of terraced houses, back to back, taking up every possible inch. Made of stone, they all looked the same with no spaces anywhere. It was only looking up at the mountains that Benjamin felt the closeness of nature. This was where he was going to live! He had never seen so many people! Even on the biggest farms at harvest, there was nothing to compare with these numbers. Men and women everywhere and shops and chapels!

He was taken to his lodgings – his home until his earnings could allow him to return. Benjamin was no stranger to hardship but this was different. When he began his first shift, he found it all so strange and frightening. All the men assembled together at the top before going down in their cages to spend the day hacking away in the seams, deep in the bowels of the earth with hardly any light. Accidents of some sort were happening all the time. He thought about the fresh air, the sun and the sea of home but knew that he just had to persevere. Some of the other colliers were from Pembrokeshire and it was good to talk to them about the old, familiar places.

Benjamin kept his spirits up. He knew that his work was keeping his family at home as he sent regular money orders from the Post Office. He built up close bonds with the other miners and their families and, on Sundays, he was able to worship at the Welsh Baptist Chapel, knowing that Margaret and the children were doing the same thing back home.

Margaret, herself, was so grateful for the money from the husband she might not see for years. She had her new baby – a little girl called MaryAnn. The child brought her comfort in Benjamin's absence even though she had to bury his mother, Anne, in the same year. Eighteen months later, Margaret had to face tragedy again and this time she was alone. Little MaryAnn died.

Margaret knew that she had to count her blessings. Yes, she had now lost three of her children – but she still had six left. They were good children and the oldest, Sarah, had moved out to live at the large house, Bristgarn, where she was working as a farm servant. She was so good to her mother, too, giving generously from her small wages. Sometimes, it was 10 shillings a week for Margaret and sometimes £1, leaving very little for herself. Soon, the other children began working too. By the time their youngest son, Harry, was fourteen and working as a servant, Benjamin came home with enough savings to provide a bit of security. At last, he was united with his family and free to feel the wind and the sun against his face in the daylight.

Gweddi Margaret Griffiths

Bendithia fy ngwaedu
Bendithia fy niffyg gwaedu
Bendithia fy mabi
Bendithia'r babanod sy'n byw 'da Ti
Bendithia'r babanod sy'n bwy 'da fi
Bendithia fy ngwaedu
Bendithia fi.

Margaret Griffiths' Prayer

Bless my bleeding
Bless my lack of bleeding
Bless my baby
Bless the babies who live with Thee
Bless the babies who live with me
Bless my bleeding
Bless me.

Benjamin and Margaret retired to a little terraced cottage in the nearby town of Fishguard. When Margaret died there in 1912, Benjamin returned to Goodwick to spend his final days with his oldest daughter, Sarah. The two parents had been extremely proud of the love and loyalty shown to them by their six children. Would life be kind to Sarah, John, Phoebe, David, William and Harry?

SARAH REES (née GRIFFITHS), born 1877

Benjamin and Margaret Griffiths' oldest child, Sarah, spent the first six years of her life in the remote but beautiful surroundings of Bwchdu and, with younger siblings arriving at the rate of one a year, she was already helping at home before the family moved. Once she had learned how to dress herself, she was showing her little brothers and sister how to do the same. In 1883, it was Sarah who helped to keep an eye on the younger children as the family made its way up to their new home in Castell. Old enough to be aware of how hard life was for her parents, she was a conscientious girl who had been introduced to the harsh realities of life very quickly. At the age of eleven, she was ready to work for a living and Sarah moved out of the tiny home to live and work at Bristgarn – a large house in the parish of Llanwnda. Her childhood was over. Times were so hard with her father away and Sarah was more than happy to give most of her small wage to her mother.

As she became a young woman, it was impossible at first to consider her own personal life and her duty to her family remained solid for some years. When her father returned from South Wales with a little money, she was freer and she courted a gentle, local man called Tomos Rees. The couple married and made their home in Cwmcelyn – a cottage a mile or so down the steep hill from Llanwnda in the area of Goodwick called Dyffryn. Its walls were made of local, greyish-brown Pembrokeshire stone that was whitewashed twice a year and its floors were earthen. Apart from the open fire that was permanently alight, Sarah needed regular amounts of water for drinking and all the household tasks. Cwmcelyn (Holly Valley) had a little bit of land that was covered in the evergreen trees that gave it its name and made it permanently dark even in summer-time. But it had a *pistyll* (a running well) which made life much easier. This easily-accessible water not only provided the family's needs but also served much of the village.

For the rest of her long life, Sarah seldom strayed far from Goodwick and Cwmcelyn – the home where she reared her five children. There were five hungry mouths to feed but the children would soon grow and take their turn in working and helping.

During her first pregnancy, a few of the women in the family wondered if she was carrying twins and Sarah, herself, thought they might be right so, when her time came, she was not too surprised to see two babies enter the world. Sons were such a blessing and all seemed to be well with the two newcomers who were called Glyn and Jack. However, as Sarah continued to nurse them, she was troubled about Glyn. He was a bit more limp and floppy than he should have been and there was something strange about his eyes. Someone mentioned the word 'mongol'. With heavy but loving hearts, Sarah and Thomas accepted that their little son had problems and everything was done to help him. They had plenty of water from the *pistyll* in the garden but they were close to the shore and sea-water was well-known for its healing properties. For the first seven years of his life, Glyn had a daily sea-water bath in his own home as relatives and neighbours took it in turns to carry a bucket down to fill it with the precious brine. The sea was only a mile away but the return journey was hard enough with the full pail carefully carried so that the water wouldn't splash out and spill. Did it help? At least the disabled child was aware of the love that surrounded him. Glyn grew to be big and strong but his serious problems remained; he was clumsy, unable to speak clearly and his behaviour became more and more erratic.

His twin, Jack, grew robustly too and was pleased when he had his first pair of long trousers made. This was a big event as it signalled the beginning of manhood – and the extra cloth was expensive. Sarah and Tomos didn't want to exclude Glyn so they decided to fit him out with a pair of long trousers too. He hated them and, in a fit of anger, took a pair of scissors and slashed the newly tailored cloth at the knee. He had made his point and wore short trousers for the rest of his life.

What did the people of Goodwick make of the family's misfortune? Sarah tried to confine Glyn to Cwmcelyn but he was crafty and often made his way down into the village. Superstitions were rife and there were all sorts of beliefs around concerning conception and pregnancy. Had poor Sarah done something out of place? Had she conceived when the moon was full – or waning? Had she stepped on something accidentally that had affected her baby in the womb?

The custom of the *ceffyl pren* (wooden horse) was dying out in rural Wales when Sarah and Tomos were newly-married but its ethos lived on informally – especially in tightly-knit, country places. The *ceffyl pren* was a way for a local community to take the law into its own hands whenever it saw or heard anything that they considered wrong. The locals humiliated the wrong-doer by turning up at his house with his effigy carried on a wooden pole and they beat saucepans together at the same time to draw everyone's attention to the culprit. A similar mentality was still active in Dyffryn and Goodwick and anybody who criticised the family or scorned Glyn was silenced.

By this time, Sarah had had three more children – another son, Thomas Henry and two daughters, Nan and Millie.

It was obvious that Glyn was going to remain dependent and Jack, who was close to his twin brother, seemed content to stay at home as the younger children were growing up. But then War was declared in 1939 and the family's existence was thrown into chaos and ripped apart. Glyn, of course, was exempt, but Jack was forced into the fray as was Thomas Henry, who was little more than a boy. Neither of them had ventured away from the confines of Cwmcelyn and Goodwick but, suddenly, they had to travel way beyond their village to strange places with names that were totally alien. And then they were taught how to fight and kill and put the lessons into practice. Their small, rural way of life had changed into one of bloody warfare as they were forced to use tactics of hatred. They witnessed horrors too awful to bear.

Jack and Thomas Henry both returned from the War alive but they remained its victims for life. Thomas Henry, a gentle and pleasant young man, was shot and returned to Cwmcelyn. He went to work in a Brickworks' factory that had opened in Goodwick. When he died in 1954, at the age of forty-one, it was difficult to know whether the war-wounds or the inhalation of dust at the Brickworks had been responsible for his death.

Jack also returned from the War to work in the Brickworks. Life had been tough for Jack. He had that acute affinity with Glyn that is often found in twins and he had taken some of his brother's suffering onto himself. His own needs as a baby and toddler were inevitably overshadowed by those of Glyn who needed so much time and attention. Then, Jack had been separated from his twin and all his close family to face the horrors of the battlefield. These things collectively took a toll on his health and Jack was prone to bouts of heavy drinking which made him an unreliable employee. He remained poorly equipped to deal with life, never married and never left his birth-place – Cwmcelyn.

Poor Sarah! Through no fault of their own, none of the four men in her life were able to give her sustained support. Her husband, Tomos, died early. Her son, Thomas Henry, died in early middle-age. Jack and Glyn lived longer but they were both fragile. Glyn made an awkward movement one day and fell into the open fire. He was badly burned and, as there was a National Health Service by this time, efforts were made to get Glyn to hospital. Jack clung onto his twin, unable to bear the thought of parting from him and Glyn died in his arms. Jack himself died two years later.

Sarah had two daughters, Nan and Millie, who were very different in personality but united in their loyalty to their mother. Nan remained in the area, married a local man and had two children. Millie also stayed in Goodwick, married another local man and had two children. Sarah had unfailing comfort, solace and support from them both.

I remember Auntie Sarah and her family well!

We used to walk down a little road and pass under a bridge before coming to the path that led to Cwmcelyn. It was always dark there with the evergreen trees all around it and I was more than a little scared! Fear is a powerful thing and I think that part of my apprehension was about meeting the unusual family inside. If the entrance was shadowy, it was no lighter when we stepped inside the cottage with its small windows and lack of electricity.

Auntie Sarah herself was thin, gaunt and pale. Over her dress, she always wore a cotton apron printed with tiny flowers all over it and sewn at the edges with bias binding. There was a small hole at one side of the apron at waist-level for a thin length of material to poke through and tie up neatly in a bow at the back with another piece of cloth. Auntie Sarah had the most dramatic face I had ever seen, with such deeply sunken, deathly-black eye-sockets that it wasn't easy to see the eyes themselves. When I did glimpse them, I noticed how dark, sharp, alert and glinting they were. Her cheekbones were prominent with the ivory flesh drawn tight across them before the skin plunged in above her jaw-bone. Auntie Sarah never smiled but was always eager to talk about very serious things to any grown-up around. Sometimes, the painful discussions were whispered and everybody shook their heads in sympathy. I never understood what all the chats were about but I could pick up the pain that loomed heavy in the room. Auntie Sarah was a widow but the house was never empty and I was glad about that because she seemed so sad. Although she never spoke to me directly, I always felt accepted.

Glyn frightened me. No-one had explained his condition and I simply couldn't understand why this stocky little man wore short trousers, why he couldn't talk properly and why he dribbled. My mother and I met him once in Goodwick when he had escaped the confines of Cwmcelyn. He sidled up to her and stumbled out the words that I could scarcely decipher, saying, "Got a fag, Nance?" My mother instantly reached into her handbag and gave him a couple of her cigarettes and was rewarded with a very wet kiss. She laughed and was obviously delighted to have pleased him. "I like old Glyn!" she said affectionately. I just felt glad that he hadn't kissed me. I'm sorry that I never understood.

I didn't get to know Jack. He was sometimes at home in Cwmcelyn but, like Auntie Sarah, he didn't speak directly to me. When he disappeared out of the room, the serious whispers began again.

Thomas Henry was a lovely, gentle man who seemed genuinely interested in me and understood my quiet ways so that I could trust him and not be afraid to speak. Sensitive, shy children always remember gentleness in adults.

Nan was like a younger version of her mother. Thin, pale and severe, her dark hair was pulled back under her beret. She'd come into Cwmcelyn, talk to Auntie Sarah, do whatever business she had to do with a no-nonsense briskness, then, sharp as a bird, she'd be gone. I played with Nan's children sometimes but it was with Millie and her family that I spent the most time.

Millie – warm, kind and sociable, enjoyed my mother's company. They were two of a kind and, as the two women chatted, I played with her young daughter and baby son.

One day we stayed to tea. My appetite was poor and I was very choosy about food so a shared meal in a strange place always worried me. I relaxed when I saw some old favourites being placed on the table but then, to my horror, Millie brought in a huge crab. She was beaming and my mother's eyes lit up so this was obviously some sort of a treat. Did people really eat crabs?

Millie turned to me and asked happily "Would you like some?"

My reply was swift and solemn. "No, thank you!"

As I ate my bread and butter, I watched the proceedings in amazement. The crab was on a plate in pride of place in the middle of the table. Was it dead or alive, I wondered? I couldn't really tell. Its pink-red shell looked very angry so it was probably alive. Did crabs have feelings? And did these feelings disappear when they died? Where did they disappear to? The grown-ups snatched away bits of the crab with their fingers until it snapped into pieces. Then they fiddled about until something like a slug came out. That was the bit they ate with noisy sucking and when the slimy bit had been swallowed, they threw the hard bits back onto the plate. I had never seen anything like it! Everyone was enjoying themselves but I just felt sorry for the crab. Good job there had been bread and butter and cake!

JOHN GRIFFITHS, born 1878

John was the second child and first son for Benjamin and Margaret Griffiths. He was content to follow the simple ways of his parents and didn't ask for much from anyone. However, life was to ask a lot from *him*. As an adult, he moved to a nearby village and married; the couple had six children.

At first, it seemed as if nothing would disrupt their basic lifestyle but, in 1914, every family in the country was disturbed by the news that the First World War had begun. John's generation had been forced to enter that bloodiest of battles in the belief that it would result in lasting peace. But, then, with their children growing up, he and his wife AnnMary, had the distress of watching their own sons go out to fight in the Second World War. Few people survived without some kind of physical or psychological damage and the burden that John and his family had to bear was particularly difficult. Their son, David John, had gone to fight in the War and returned home to Britain on leave. Can young people be trained to fight and develop skills in cold killing – and then switch that aggression off like a tap? Probably not! It was an irony that, away from the front-line, David John was murdered. What a long-lasting and sinister legacy War leaves! Does a family ever recover from such a trauma? Probably not!

PHOEBE GRIFFITHS, born 1879

Phoebe's early years were similar to those of her older sister and brother. She was born at Bwchdu with the sound of the sea whistling in its draughts under the cottage door. She was already helping out with simple tasks by the time the family moved up to Castell when she was four years old. Phoebe went to the elementary school at Henner before leaving Castell to become a servant at Penrhiw – another of the large houses in the Parish of Llanwnda. She remained there throughout her working life, never married, and, by the time she retired as a respected, senior housekeeper, her employers showed their indebtedness by endowing her with a small pension. Retirement posed a particular problem as she had nowhere to live but her youngest brother, Harry, returned to Goodwick to provide her with a home.

There was nothing of note, then, in this woman's life – but Phoebe's experiences of tough living produced a few surprising gifts.

I remember Auntie Phoebe well!

Her appearance was severe and totally uncompromising. Her hair, though grey, still retained a bit of its original brown and its waves were firmly tied back into a tiny bun at the nape of her neck. I only saw Auntie Phoebe laugh once. The joke was about peeling potatoes.

The first thing I noticed about the face that had never worn make-up and always been exposed to the country air, was her deep wrinkles. They were there all the time but moved into different patterns whenever there was any movement. Like watching ripples in a pond, new designs came about whenever she talked, sighed, sniffed or frowned. Auntie Phoebe's face was brown and awesome but if I did manage to focus on her eyes, I saw that they were sharp, dark and sparkling.

Her clothes were sombre in design and colour – greys and dark browns that were usually covered by a cotton apron for working. Having spent all her life in service, she continued being a housekeeper well into her eighties in the home that Harry had provided for her. It was too established a habit to break. She was often seen polishing the furniture or scampering up the very steep garden to fetch some vegetables or herbs – but Auntie Phoebe came into her own in the kitchen. She had no small talk and was most at ease discussing the food that she grew, collected or prepared. She knew everything that was to be known about potatoes – the old ones, the new ones, the varieties, the blights, when to scrape and when to peel.

She made no concessions whatsoever to her age when she was well into her eighties. One day, she set off to pick blackberries. Donning her coat and hat, she knew exactly where to find the juiciest and ripest fruits and was determined to come back with a bagful for tarts and jam. Concern was expressed when Auntie Phoebe failed to return at the expected time but she eventually arrived home with her bounty, undeterred. The delay had happened because she had fallen in the river. After the fall, she just continued her fruit-picking in her wet clothes. With an irritated frown, the wrinkles danced around her face as she complained about the waste of time.

Auntie Phoebe was an expert weather-forecaster and I never failed to be amazed at her method and the accurate results. As a child on a seaside holiday, I always hoped that the next day would bring sunshine so that we could all go to the beach. She was the person to ask about this! In the kitchen, she had some seaweed hanging up from the ceiling and this was the source of her weather-forecasting. She went up to the hanging plant and studied the seaweed from every angle. What could she possibly see in this long brown-green weed that still smelt of the sea? There'd be a pause before the touching began. With her bronzed, worn hands, she felt the seaweed all over – the bulbous bits and the leafy pieces. As she was doing *this, the wrinkles on her face moved and curved and we knew that she would have reached her verdict when they settled again. The whole process was unhurried and it was with the minimum of words that she let us into the secret. "Tomorrow will be fine," she'd say, or "After rain in the morning, it'll be clear!" Auntie Phoebe's predictions were never wrong.*

It was in the kitchen again that she performed her most unexpected gift. She did it in secret and no-one was allowed to intrude whilst she was in action. There used to be a competition in a Sunday newspaper called 'Spot the Ball'. It featured a photograph of a football match in action but the crucial ball was missing. The winner was the person who could correctly guess where the ball should be by marking the place with a cross. The people running the competition obviously chose unusual and unexpected ball positions which were not evident from the players' positions and stance. Now, Auntie Phoebe had never played football; she had never seen a professional game. The only experience she had was seeing impromptu matches up in Llanwnda during the Christmas-tide festivities – yet Auntie Phoebe won this competition not just once but several times. She received very generous money prizes which must have been a revelation for someone who had spent her life as a servant and housekeeper. She never revealed the secret of her skill to anyone!

DAVID GRIFFITHS, born 1879

David was the last of the Griffiths' children to be born at Bwchdu and had no memories of it. For him, Castell was the childhood home.

Again, in his early years, he followed the same pattern as his siblings and, as a young man, he was faced with the same dilemma as his brothers. Should he struggle to try to work on the land at a time when the prospect for labourers was so poor, wait for new opportunities in the area – or should he leave its uncertain familiarity altogether and try to make a life for himself in the booming industrial South?

It certainly looked as if there were going to be jobs for men in Fishguard soon. In 1904, when David was fifteen, two million tons of rock were blasted in Pencw, very close to their home. No-one had seen anything like it and certainly no-one had *heard* anything like it! The sound went on and on for months as spasmodic explosions disrupted the peace of the countryside and disturbed the animals. The local men working on the rock were afraid as they carefully placed explosive in the rock and made a fast retreat before the stone was spewed out in pieces! What was happening? There were great plans to develop Fishguard as an international harbour so the rock, mixed with the sand from Goodwick beach, was being used to build a new railway station and breakwater. Yes, it seemed as if this would bring work to the area – but David decided not to wait.

His father, Benjamin, had gone down to the South and David decided to follow in his footsteps. He settled in Glamorganshire and worked underground as a miner. He married a local girl, Lisa, and the couple had four children but when she was weaning her youngest, Lisa needed something to help dry up her milk supply. She asked the advice of a local 'wise woman' who recommended saltpetre. Lisa took the saltpetre, was poisoned by it and died. David was left, widowed, with a dangerous job, long working hours and four young children to support single-handed.

At a later date, there was to be a close link with Uncle David's family – but not for another generation!

THOMAS GRIFFITHS (1883-4), WILLIAM GRIFITHS born 1885, and JAMES GRIFFITHS (1886-8)

Margaret Griffiths had three more sons in the space of four years. Little Thomas Griffiths lived for just one year. Two years after his death, another brother, James Griffiths, was born and he lived for two years. Williams Griffith, born in 1885 between the two unfortunate brothers, survived.

WILLIAM GRIFFITHS at Stop-and-Call

As a lad, William had little memory of his father and was only able to get to know him in adolescence when he returned to Pembrokeshire.

When he became a man, William married a local girl, Catherine, and the couple lived in Stop-and-Call – a tiny hamlet between Llanwnda and Goodwick. Theirs was another tiny, white-washed home with very limited facilities, its back facing the steep hill down to the sea. It was here that Catherine had her babies and the couple raised ten children. How did they manage in such a tiny home with little income? They didn't ask such questions but just got on with the job. There was Gwyneth, Phoebe Ann, Owen, Danny, Nell, Bronwen, Denzil, Ronald, Phyllis and Betty! By the time the youngest children were born, the older ones were already working and farm labouring was not the only option anymore as local industries had been introduced. Apart from the Brickworks in Goodwick, the Harbour was bringing jobs for the men with the beginnings of a tourist trade.

It was a happy home where everyone was loved in spite of the cramped accommodation. All their hardships were eclipsed by the heartache of the Second World War. It was a familiar story. William and Catherine had known the tremendous losses incurred in the first of these Wars and now their children were going to be subjected to the horrors of the Second one.

Even though the Penny Post had arrived, there were few letters sent and received in places like Llanwnda and Stop-and-Call. Telegrams were even rarer and, in wartime, they meant only one thing. The couple were terrified when the postman arrived one day. They trembled as they opened the telegram which told them that their son, Danny, was missing, presumed drowned at sea. In a way, this was worse than knowing that Danny had been killed. The word 'presumed' left feelings raw and confused. They couldn't have a funeral, there was no body, there was always the chance that he would be found. Would he return one day to the cottage and open the door with a smile and say, "Hullo, Mam! Hullo, Dad!" A gypsy woman happened to be in the area some time later and she told the distraught parents that Danny had not died but was 'wandering the earth'. If this information was meant to ease their pain, it failed miserably. The agony was unbearable. All the family suffered but William was haunted by it all and he became ill.

Nothing and no-one seemed to be able to help him as his health worsened and he became weaker and weaker. He began to bleed from his ears, his nose and his mouth. They said he died of a broken heart. It seems as good a diagnosis as anything else. As a widow, Catherine remained at the cottage in Stop-and-Call but she was never alone. This was hardly surprising with nine surviving children and, when they, in their turn, married, they produced another generation – a generation of hope for the future.

I remember Auntie Catherine and her family well.

We often went up to visit her in her little cottage. The road up to Stop-and-Call was perilously steep and seemed further than the mile or two in distance from Goodwick. After all the energy that was needed to reach it, a rest was needed. And there was nowhere better to stop and call than at Auntie Catherine's.

She was another old, old woman wearing sombre clothes and living in a dark home. The outside of the cottage was immaculate and glittering with its whitewashed walls but there was no lighting indoors and the windows were very small. Auntie Catherine was always pleased to see us and it wasn't long before the tin of biscuits came out to be offered around with the cup of tea. The tin was passed from one person to the next and, as I looked inside, I never knew what would be there to place on my little china plate. Sometimes there were biscuits and sometimes there were small cakes. I chose something out of the tin and passed it on.

There was one thing that worried me about the cottage. My mother had spoken about the picture of Jesus on the wall. Apparently, the eyes followed you around. I found myself looking up at it again and again and, yes, the eyes did seem to follow me. If I moved to pass the biscuit tin on, they were looking at me; when I sat back in my chair, they were still looking at me. How could this be? Were they really looking at all the other people in the room at the same time? Was Jesus cross with us or was he pleased? Wasn't Auntie Catherine scared to live in that room with those eyes watching everything she did? I couldn't work it out and I couldn't help looking and looking again to check whether I was still being watched or not.

Apart from the fear of this picture, I enjoyed myself at the cottage and met many of the nine children. There was Owen with his lovely smile who was gentle, quiet, unassuming and always wanted to please. Ronald was chatty and outgoing, with a joke ready to share or a story to tell. Betty, the youngest daughter, was pretty, gentle and kind.

But the person we saw most of was Phoebe Ann and her family. Phoebe Ann was the second of William and Catherine's children and she married a local man, Tommy. A gently charismatic man, Tommy built the house that was to be their married home half-way up the steep hill between Stop-and-Call and Goodwick. I could never get over the fact that Tommy had built it himself and at such a sharp angle. It was so clever! From this house, there was a clear and panoramic view of the sea that stretched to the little coves beyond Fishguard to Newport and Cardigan Bay. Phoebe Ann was very much a 'Griffiths' woman with her short stature, very dark hair, pale complexion and those brown, shining eyes that laughed or were easily moved to tears. I loved being with her and her family.

She and Tommy had two daughters and I played a lot with Sylvia, who was a year or so younger than me. The older sister, Janet, was several years older than me at a time when those few years made a big difference. Janet wore make-up and she had a boy-friend. She also had an interesting story to tell which concerned her autograph book; she brought it out obligingly to show me every time. In 1956, the film Moby Dick was made in and around Fishguard. Big Hollywood stars featured in the film – including Gregory Peck. Although people were delighted and excited to have such an event happening locally, there was some concern about where to house the cast whilst the film was being made. The prestigious Fishguard Bay Hotel had been built to cater for all the rich clientèle expected when the Harbour was developed as an internationally renowned port; these grand plans didn't materialise and the Hotel had fallen into disrepair. There was a scramble to upgrade it, paint the walls and enrol local people to work there during the screening. Janet was taken on as a chambermaid. The film was not without its excitement for the rubber whale managed to float away and was never seen again! When the film was eventually completed, Janet asked Gregory Peck if he would sign his name in her autograph book before he disappeared. He offered her more than his signature – he gave her the scar that he had worn in the film. I loved to look at it with its realistic, hardened blood and a couple of stray hairs!

Sylvia, the younger sister, and I had a lot of fun together. We had a game that we played as often as we could afford. We walked down to the Harbour whenever an Irish ferry boat was in and approached the vessel. With aplomb and dramatic skills worthy of RADA, we found a sailor and asked him if he would show us round the boat. No sailor ever refused us and we followed him, as, with great interest, we asked intelligent questions. "How many cabins are there?" one of us would venture, "and how many passengers do you carry?" We waited for a moment to absorb the information that we had heard many times before we continued the questioning. "How long does the voyage take?" or "Is Rosslare the only Harbour you use in Ireland?" – and so on. By the time we had exhausted *the man, we made a graceful departure, handing him a sixpenny piece tip and exclaiming, "That was most enjoyable!" I'm sure we convinced no-one but, if the sailors never refused to show us round, they never refused the sixpenny tip either. As soon as we were out of their sight, we collapsed into hysterical laughter. When one of us stopped giggling, the other started up again and we were helpless. Oh, it was well worth sixpence!*

HENRY GRIFFITHS, born 1887, and MARYANN GRIFFITHS (1890-92)

Henry was the youngest son for Benjamin and Margaret Griffiths. He was a healthy baby, born in Pontiago, Llanwnda, in 1887 – the family all called him Harry. When Harry was three years old, a baby sister, MaryAnn, arrived. She was to be the last child in the family, born just after Benjamin had left to work in the coal-mines – but she only lived for two years.

Harry went to the local elementary school in Henner as his brothers and sisters had done. He was a particularly gifted pupil, quick to learn – and he dreamed dreams! The reality of the situation, though, was that the family was struggling to survive and, by 1901, at the age of fourteen, Harry, too, had followed the pattern set by his older brothers and sisters. He had left home to be a servant at Ffynnondruidion Farm which had once employed his mother. Any plans or hopes of a better life were on hold until the family's fortunes were more stable – and Harry was happy to do that because he was a loyal young man, close to his mother. When he was eventually freer, he decided to go to the South to work in the coal industry. His father, Benjamin, had gone there and so had his brother, David. Now it was Harry's turn.

There was nothing attractive about the idea of mining underground apart from the opportunity to earn a little money. It was the only way out for people from the rural agricultural areas who only had limited formal education behind them. Even the chance to earn some money was not an immediate asset. Initially, like his father, Harry had to share a rented room as a lodger. He had gone to the small town of Abercynon and his first years were hard. He had *heard* about the dark pits, the cage, the danger, but experiencing it first-hand was a different matter. It was difficult to be robbed of the daylight. His wages were low in the beginning and he had to pay the rent as well as send some money back to his sister, Sarah, who was taking care of their ageing father. Harry had to be patient but, in due course, he was able to rent rooms just for himself. This was exactly what he had been waiting for! His father had had to leave his mother, Margaret, at home in Llanwnda with the children but Harry wanted to bring his fiancée to Abercynon to be with him. So, when he returned to Pembrokeshire, it was to marry.

Early in the year of 1914, with the ground still wintry-hard, Harry went back to Llanwnda and, from there, he and his family made their way to Maenclochog. He entered Horeb Baptist Chapel and stood nervously but proudly at the front. He had been able to provide good living quarters for his bride and he could support her financially when the children came. Henry was the happiest man in the world when he saw the stunningly beautiful Jane Lloyd come into the chapel. How had she acquired her serenity and dignified posture?

JANE LLOYD

I didn't have the privilege of meeting my grandmother, Jane Lloyd.

There are just two photographs of her. In the first one, she is seen as an extremely beautiful and gracious young lady. The second picture shows a married woman with her husband and first child. The mother's hands are worn but she still has a wonderful beauty and air of gentility.

Everyone who knew her spoke of her exquisite good looks and her lovely, loving nature. She liked the feel of silk – especially the delicate shantung silk that had to be bone dry when ironed. And Jane Lloyd was not deprived of those silk clothes to wear.

The Landed Gentry

As a child, I had known Jane Lloyd's elderly sister. I can remember one of Jane's nieces and one of her nephews. They, too, had died by the time I reached adulthood so I had very little knowledge about Jane Lloyd's background. Admittedly, I had gathered together some census returns, birth, marriage and death certificates but these faced me coldly on the page. How could I begin to understand something about this gracious woman who was my grandmother – and the people from whom she was descended?

I had a pleasant surprise ahead of me!

★

My husband, Peter, was driving along a narrow little road that seemed to be leading nowhere. There were few signs along the way on that February day in 2006 and we thought that we had taken a wrong turning. It was then that I saw the sign. 'Colston Farm'. "That's it!" I exclaimed. "That's where they lived!"

It seemed such an unlikely mission and Peter stayed in the car as I followed a track to the farmhouse. I noticed an elderly lady and asked if she knew anything about the Lloyd family. "Yes!" she said. "Martha

Lloyd lived in the bungalow down there"

"Did you know her?" I asked. "Oh, yes – and her sisters!"

I thanked her and returned to the car to tell Peter that I had found something. Patiently, he listened as we drove into the village of Little Newcastle and on to our destination in Goodwick. My mother-in-law was seriously ill at the time and we had decided to have a few days away but, in the early hours of the morning, we were summoned back as she had deteriorated in hospital.

I reflected on the brief meeting with the lady at the farm. I checked up on the census returns and discovered that Martha Lloyd was my great-great-aunt – the sister of my great grandfather who was Jane Lloyd's father. This aunt couldn't have lived in a bungalow in the nineteenth century, surely? Because my mother-in-law was so ill, I knew that I wouldn't have the chance to visit again in the foreseeable future so I wrote a letter to Colston Farm, asking the woman if she had any more memories. A few days later, a letter arrived in the post from someone called Richard Davies. The farmer's wife had handed my letter to him and he was replying on her behalf. Richard turned out to be a historian who had been born and bred in the village of Little Newcastle and was gifted with an encyclopaedic knowledge of the area. He was also distantly related to me. The letter read:

Today, Mrs. Brenda Evans of Colston Farm handed me your letter with the queries about the Lloyd family. I am pleased to tell you that we can help you and that we can take the pedigree back many generations …

William Lloyd married Jane Bennett, who was his second cousin. William was the grandson of Mary Lloyd and Jane was the grand-daughter of Mary Lloyd's sister, Elizabeth Bennett. Mary Lloyd, Elizabeth Bennett and their unmarried sister, Ann Symmons were the co-heiresses of John Symmons. The Symmons' had been resident in the parish of Little Newcastle since the days of the first Queen Elizabeth.

The GRIFFITHS family

David GRIFFITHS m. **Anne**
b.1812 Hayscastle b.1812 Llandissilio
Ag. Labourer

Thomas JENKINS m. **Phoebe DAVIES**
b.1806 Llanwnda b.1813 Fishguard
Ag. Labourer

John	Owen
b.1845	1848

Daniel	Anne	David	John	William	Sarah	Jane
b.1832	1834	1838	1847	1849	1853	1859

Benjamin GRIFFITHS b. 1844 ... m. — — — — ... **Margaret JENKINS.** b. 1851
Llanhowel Ag. Labourer/Coal-miner Llanwnda

Sarah	John	Phoebe	David	Thomas	William	James	MaryAnn
b1877	1878	1879	1870	1883-4	1885	1886-8	1892-4

Henry GRIFFITHS — m. — **Jane LLOYD** b.1887
b. 1887 Llanwnda
Farm servant/ coal-miner/businessman

Peggy	Gwenllian Lloyd	Catherine	Mildred Morgan	**Phoebe Ann Henner**	William	Benjamin	Owen	Nesta May	Georgina
b. 1914		1916		**GRIFFITHS** b. 1919		1921			1923
m. Philip ADDINGTON				m. .Lewis William WILLIAMS.		m Olga Wright			m. William Owen

Howard	Heather Jane

Graham	Tara Jane	Megan Ruth	Eleri Mair	Dafydd Wyn

Diana Gruffydd WILLIAMS m. **Peter Huw MORGAN**

Rhiannon Meleri Llinos MORGAN m. **Huw John DAVIES**

Bethan Nia DAVIES **Catrin Elinor DAVIES**

*Bwchdu Cottage, 2006. Bwchdu was Benjamin and Margaret Griffiths'
first home in 1876. Uninhabited since 1950, it has many of the original
features. This photograph shows the half-loft.*

Fishguard Square. Taken at about the time when Benjamin Griffiths left his native Pembrokeshire. (Photograph: 'Reflective Images', Port Talbot)

Henry Griffiths (Data) as a young man.

Auntie Sarah at Cwmcelyn with me (in sailor suit) and my cousin, Janice.

Jane Lloyd as a young woman.

The LLOYD family

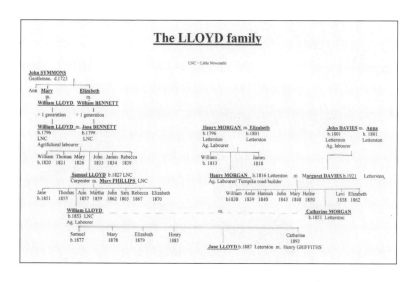

LNC = Little Newcastle

John SYMMONS
Gentleman. d.1723

Ann	**Mary**		**Elizabeth**
	m.		m.
	William LLOYD		**William BENNETT**
	+ 1 generation		+ 1 generation

William LLOYD m. **Jane BENNETT** — **Henry MORGAN** m. **Elizabeth** — **John DAVIES** m. **Anna**
b.1796 / b.1799 — b.1796 / b.1801 — b.1801 / b. 1801
LNC / LNC — Letterston / Letterston — Letterston / Letterston
Agrifultural labourer — Ag. Labourer — Ag. labourer

William Thomas Mary | John James Rebecca — William | James
b.1820 1821 1826 | 1833 1834 1839 — b. 1813 | 1818

Samuel LLOYD b.1827 LNC — **Henry MORGAN** b.1816 Letterston m **Margaret DAVIES** b.1921 Letterston,
Carpenter m. **Mary PHILLIPS** LNC — Ag. Labourer/ Turnpike road builder

Jane Thomas Ann Martha John Sara Rebecca Elizabeth — William Anne Hannah John Mary Hettie — Levi Elizabeth
b.1851 1855 1857 1859 1862 1865 1867 1870 — b1838 1839 1840 1843 1848 1850 — 1858 1862

William LLOYD ———— m. ———— **Catherine MORGAN**
b.1853 LNC — b.1851 Letterston
Ag. Labourer

Samuel Mary Elizabeth Henry — Catherine
b.1877 1878 1879 1883 — 1893

Jane LLOYD b.1887 Leterston m. Henry GRIFFITHS

The brook by Beulah Chapel, Little Newcastle. Members of the Lloyd family were baptised here by full immersion.

Martha Lloyd in front of her cottage.
(Photograph courtesy of Brenda Evans)

Henry and Jane Griffiths with their first child, Peggy, c. 1916.

John Symmons' grandfather, Thomas, had married into the Tucker family. Through the Tuckers, you can trace the ancestry back to the Wogans, who were connected to the Herberts (Earls of Pembroke and Montgomery). Through a female line, the Wogans could claim descent from Edmund Crouchback, Earl of Lancaster, Duke of Lancaster, son of Henry III.

I was staggered by my good fortune and, in the summer, Peter and I were able to go to Little Newcastle again. Richard showed us around St. Peter's Church and supplied us with a wealth of information throughout the afternoon. He took us down to see Brenda (the elderly lady I had first met at Colston) and she used her massive chapel-door key to show us where Martha Lloyd and her sister had spent their Sundays in Beulah chapel.

"Martha sat there*!" she explained specifically, "and her sister, Ann, sat* there *with her husband."*

What about this bungalow, I asked? The cottage where the Lloyd family had lived in the nineteenth century had been renovated and the current owners are none other than Brenda's own son and family!

WILLIAM and JANE LLOYD
at Little Newcastle

When little William Lloyd was born in 1796, his family had known nothing but life in the small village of Little Newcastle. They were steeped in its history and taught William to be proud of his roots. In 1799, just before the dawn of a new century, William's second cousin, Jane Bennett, was born and the family continued to teach the little ones about local events that had carved their own mark in history.

Just across from the village green where the motte had once stood, was St. Peter's Church where the font had been in place since the twelfth-century. William and Jane knew it well. They were told about the pilgrims who had stopped here on their way to St. David's and taken advantage of the local wells. They learnt that St. Peter's Church had originally been dedicated to St. David so they understood its ancient Celtic connections. As for the precious solid silver chalice, it had been there since the time of Queen Elizabeth I! Little Newcastle might be a small place but its people had welcomed many great men into their own church. John Wesley had preached here in 1770 and, with the people thirsty for more of his inspiration, he had returned in 1784. William and Jane knew some of the wonderful hymns written by William Williams of Pantycelyn – and *he* too had come to Little Newcastle. As for Howel Harries, he had to abandon the church altogether and address the crowd outside on the village green because of the huge crowds assembled to hear his words. Some said that they were ten thousand in number!

As William Lloyd grew to be a man and Jane Bennett blossomed into maturity, the young couple realised that they were in love. A wedding was arranged and there was no need for their families to assess each other for suitability. Jane and William's grandmothers were sisters. Relations smiled and offered their blessings at the marriage service and the cows and sheep in the fields outside also seemed to be adding their own voices to honour this union. These were the animals that William helped to tend for he was an agricultural labourer. He and his new wife had not benefited from their ancestors' estates.

Although William and Jane had lost out personally on land ownership, they knew that they had plenty of generous support from the more fortunate members in the family. They began their married life working on Whitehall Farm that belonged to Jane's brother, Samuel.

Over the years, Samuel Bennett was very good to William and Jane and in 1841, he had their oldest son living in a loft over one of his stables. It was not a bad place for a young lad to live – with the warmth from the animals, a comfortable straw bed, a bit of independence and the loft-songs to enjoy with friends and family at the end of a long working day. William and Jane themselves were now middle-aged and still had their six youngest children living with them.

Ten years later, they were still with Samuel, working on his farm with the exotic name of 'Guadeloup'. It didn't occur to them to do anything else but accept the mixed fortunes of the seasons on the land and, when the harvest was plentiful, they wondered how anyone could want more than this simple way of life. No, there was certainly no reason to move away from this lush, gentle corner of Pembrokeshire with its mild climate! Things would carry on as they always had done for the residents in Little Newcastle! Some of the people who came in from the south of the county for the cattle fairs had been invaded in the past and they had lost their language and some of the old traditions – but this was not so for William, Jane and their families. No, nothing would change for them! Life would revolve around the hay-making, the sowing and the reaping.

Harvest-time, when all the farmers and labourers in the area co-operated to get everything finished quickly, was eagerly awaited. It was exhausting but satisfying work and there was the supper to enjoy afterwards. There was great fun as the corn was gathered in!

William went out first thing in the morning with his sons and joined the other men in the field to harvest the corn. Jane worked in the farmhouse with her sister-in-law and all the other women who were preparing the food for the men throughout the day as well as the harvest-supper that followed.

It was monotonous and taxing labour in the fields but, just before the corn was completely cropped, the men cheered up and a strange thing happened! The last tuft was left in the ground!

Sometimes it was William's job to skilfully plait that final tuft and tie it at the top with straw. Then all the men took turns to try and cut the tuft clean from the ground from a distance with their reaping-hooks. This was difficult and, when it was William's turn, he had to kneel down low on the ground like the others and hurl it. If someone *did* succeed, the field was filled with the sound of claps and cheers – but, more often than not, they had to abandon their efforts and the chief labourer of the day approached the tuft to cut it down himself. This wasn't the end of the story for there was great fun to follow!

With the tuft freed from the earth at last, all the men and lads out in the field gathered around the triumphant cutter as he began to sing the familiar words:

"Bore y codais hi," he'd chant, "Hwyr y dilynais hi,

Mi ces hi, mi ces hi"

(In the morning, I raised her, in the evening, I followed her. I *got* her, I *got* her!)

Then everyone else sang out the response with gusto.

"Beth gest ti?" (What did you get?)

and the cutter replied mischievously,

"Gwrach, gwrach, gwrach!" (a hag, a hag, a hag!)

Still laughing, the men and boys then took the tuft (*y gaseg fedi* – the harvest mare) into the farmhouse – but this was no simple matter either! The man who had cut it from the field had to hide it under his clothes so that no-one would guess who was carrying it. It was bulky so this was easier said than done and the poor man had to try to walk in towards the farmhouse with his usual gait. When this lot fell to William, his sons tried to help him – "Do it like this, Daddy!" said William and Thomas. "Carry it higher! We can see it!" added Samuel, John and James in unison. As soon as they were happy that the corn tuft was well-hidden, all the men and boys walked in together. The man with the 'secret' tried his best to walk normally and the others plodded awkwardly to try and confuse the women who were inside the farmhouse, putting the finishing touches to the harvest-supper.

Jane was with her daughters, Mary and Rebecca, and all the other women as they stopped their work for a few minutes when they heard the men approaching. They filled buckets with water and hurled them at the men who tried to duck and keep out of their firing-line. This ritual was always the same and, whilst the women were doing their best to soak the men to their skins – and especially the one they thought to be carrying the corn-tuft – the men were running around trying to get into the farmhouse dry! When they finally got inside, all was revealed to shouts of laughter and applause! If the man with the tuft had managed to get inside without getting wet, he was treated to the prize of one shilling, as much beer as he could drink and a place of honour at the harvest-supper. If the poor man had got drenched, he had to do without the beer! It was such a happy occasion and, at times like these, William and Jane counted their many blessings.

Life is full of surprises and in 1861, when William had almost reached his three score years and ten, there was a change in family circumstances which enabled him to become farmer and manager of 80 acres of land. He and Jane moved into Colston farmhouse in Little Newcastle, where they lived and employed two servants. The status was short-lived and, when William and Jane were eighty years of age, they were back in a leased cottage in the grounds of Colston as labourers. Their son, Samuel, was living next door with his young family and this was a great bonus for the elderly parents. For a short time, they had had a taste of land ownership but, in their final years, they were back working the soil and caring for the animals, surrounded by their family and still praising their God!

SAMUEL LLOYD and MARY PHILLIPS
of Little Newcastle

Samuel was born in 1827, the fourth of William and Jane Lloyd's seven children. Like his brothers and sisters, he had to help out at home and in the fields at a very early age – but Samuel needed some schooling as well because he was seeking an apprenticeship to a local carpenter. How would he get an education?

Welsh children fared well at a time when few children went to school at all. Sunday was a day of rest from work for everyone. Several services in churches and chapels were held but Sunday schools attended to more than spiritual needs. Griffith Jones of Llanddowror had been responsible for setting up circulating schools in Wales to provide tuition for the ordinary people in the winter evenings when labourers and their children usually had some spare time. There had been a circulating school in Little Newcastle but, although it had closed before Samuel was ready to take advantage of it, teaching continued in the Sunday Schools and a certain Madame Bevan had opened a school in the village. Young Samuel would be able to learn how to read, write and do arithmetic.

As a country boy, of course, he was already familiar with all the trees – he knew the ones that shed their leaves in autumn and those that kept them, he knew their shapes against the sky-line, the fruits and blossoms, the cheeky, mystic old mistletoe, the hawthorn and other trees that were trained to grow as hedges. He could recognise their diseases, knew about the conkers and the acorns, the clever little V-shaped sycamore seeds that blew across the land in the wind ready to fall and implant themselves everywhere – Samuel knew them all! There was so much more for him to discover, though, and he had new skills to master. He watched every movement the carpenter made so that he could copy it. He needed to know how to fell a tree and, of course, he had to learn the craft of fashioning it.

Samuel was very proud when his apprenticeship was over and he became a carpenter in his own right! Every community, however small, respected and needed at least one carpenter. It was his privilege and responsibility to care for every local inhabitant from the cradle to the grave. *He* was the one to design the baby's crib and *he* was the one to work on the wood that made the coffin. In such an agricultural area where simple tools were used, everyone needed to ask something of Samuel Lloyd. There were the pig troughs to be made, buckets, dairy equipment, butter churns, ploughs, carts and wheelbarrows.

On top of that, there was all the household furniture – window frames and doors were needed, chairs, tables and settles. Then, there was the challenge of making the Welsh dressers! These were often given as a dowry from a bride's family and, though the extensive and delicate carving took so long to complete, these pieces of furniture could sell for several pounds. Apart from bringing in a handsome sum of money, this was a particularly rewarding job as Samuel knew how the dressers took pride of place in people's houses. They were polished and prized and passed on to the next generation. No-one could put a price on such satisfaction!

Samuel didn't have to look far for a wife. Mary Phillips, a year younger than himself, was a native of Little Newcastle and the couple were to become another generation of Lloyds who were born, bred and buried in the village. The only move they had was from one part of the community to another. Llandoc was their first home, then, when their first children were young, they moved on to Colston. Colston was an area of Little Newcastle with a cluster of cottages around the main farm of the same name. When Samuel's parents were managing the farm itself, he and Mary came to live in the cottage next door. Its single, long, narrow room downstairs was partitioned to make two separate areas and there was a loft above for sleeping.

Samuel and Mary had a large family and, soon, the girls were spending time with their mother learning domestic skills whilst the boys followed Samuel around to learn a little bit about carpentry, local history and the land.

"Do you see those stones?" Samuel asked, as they passed the field beyond Colston farmhouse. "How old do you think they are?"

"As old as you, Dad?" the boys ventured.

Samuel's smile told them that they were wrong. "As old as Tadcu (Granddad), then?"

"No. They've been here for thousands of years!" Samuel marvelled himself at the ancient burial chambers and was pleased that the boys ran over to get a closer look.

They carried on walking up towards the main village and Samuel wasted no time with the lads. "What's that tree?" he asked, pointing ahead.

"Sycamore!"

Pembrokeshire had plenty of them and they were useful for a carpenter as they didn't crack easily. That had been an easy question for the boys and they decided to prove to their father how well they had listened.

"And that's a beech!" young William added. "It can be turned when it's still green and it's good for making bowls!"

Samuel was pleased with his sons and they all agreed that there was nothing as good as a beech bowl and spoon to eat the much-loved *cawl*. Even talking about *cawl* made the boys feel hungry!

In 1871, when Samuel was forty-four and Mary was forty-three, they still had nine children living with them and there was always so much to do! There was the house to look after, the pigs to feed, the fire to guard, the fuel to collect, the vegetables to grow, the food to be prepared and cooked, clothes to be washed in the stream, water to be fetched, pots and pans to be cleaned, butter and cheese to be made, clothes to be dried and pressed... All this – *and* Samuel's carpentry!

The Lloyds had worshipped faithfully in St. Peter's Church for generations but the religious revivals that had been sweeping through the country reached Little Newcastle in 1795. People were attracted by the charismatic appeal of the Non-Conformists and, as a result, Beulah Baptist chapel was built in 1808. Some of the family, touched by the passion of the sermons and the simplicity of the meetings, started going to Beulah and were baptised there, plunged into the chilly water of the brook that ran alongside the building. But, whether they stayed in the Church or moved to the chapel, they all knew that there was only one God, whose Son, Jesus, had come to earth for *all* humanity.

On Christmas mornings, the Lloyd family went out for a brisk walk to whet their appetites for the dinner they'd share later. What could be lovelier than this chance to meet up together and eat roasted goose with tasty vegetables and – oh, yes, there was pudding too!

Samuel and Mary looked at their children and wondered what would become of them. So many people were leaving the country life for the industries or even emigrating. But they couldn't imagine Thomas, Jane, William, Ann, Martha, John, James, Rebecca or Elizabeth ever leaving the village. Little Newcastle was their whole life and soon Samuel would be carving special items for their weddings. Surely, the only uncertainty for the Lloyds would be the venue? Would the marriages take place in St. Peter's – or Beulah?

Gweddi Samuel Lloyd

Diolch i Ti am yr hedyn a dyfa'r goeden.
Arglwydd, bydd yn ei chymygu.
Diolch i Ti am y goedyn sy'n cynnal fy nhamaid.
Arglwydd, bydd yn ei llunio.
Diolch i Ti am fy nwylaw sy'n cerfio.
Arglwydd, bydd yn ei werthu.
Diolch i Ti am y ddaear a groesawodd yr hen goeden.
Arglwydd, bydd yn yr hedyn newydd.

Samuel Lloyd's Prayer

Thank You for the seed that came before the tree.
Lord, be in its felling.
Thank You for the tree that earns my keep.
Lord, be in its crafting.
Thank You for my hands that carve.
Lord, be in its selling.
Thank You for the ground where the felled tree grew.
Lord, be in the new seed.

THE LLOYD CHILDREN
at Colston Farm Cottage

For Thomas, Jane, William, Ann, Martha, John, James, Rebecca and Elizabeth Lloyd, the family's inheritance of land was now just a tale to be told. They needed to learn how to work hard. The Lloyd girls became gifted quilters, using the traditional Welsh method of sewing three layers of material together with neat, running stitches. They followed a pattern carefully and the evenly-spaced stitches ensured that there were two 'good' sides to the quilt.

Even as elderly women, Jane (born 1851), Martha (born 1859) and Elizabeth (born 1870) could be seen quilting by the window in the parlour of their cottage at Colston. By this time, their eyesight didn't have to struggle with the limited light that came from the window – they had the new oil-lamps! They no longer had to guess the time – there was a wall-clock to tell them the hour. As they sat on the oak chairs made by their father, Samuel, the sisters enjoyed each other's company, settling close to the light, concentrating on the stitching, chatting about old times and often singing the hymns they knew so well. And, when the quilts were complete, they had the pleasure of knowing that their dear ones would be kept warm on winter nights.

ANN JAMES (née LLOYD)

Ann Lloyd married a local man called James James. The couple stayed in Little Newcastle but moved into their own house higher up in the village nearer the church – not far from the home of Barti Ddu, the notorious pirate. Ann was a devout member of Beulah Chapel and made her way down there regularly in her clogs with a shawl wrapped round her to keep out the cold wind and rain. One Sunday night in bed, Ann got up and was amazed to see a powerful light ahead of her and she spoke excitedly to her husband. "Cwyd, Siemi!" she began, "Mae'r Iesu yn dod ar gymylau'r nef!" ('Look, Jamie, Jesus is coming on the clouds of Heaven!') *This* was the moment all Christian people had been waiting for – but the couple couldn't hear the trumpet accompanying the Second Coming. The Return in Glory had actually been the searchlight from the area around Pembroke Dock.

Ann and James had three children who all left their familiar, rural village. Their daughter and one of their sons moved to London; the other son made that bold journey across the seas to the New World of America.

MARTHA LLOYD

Martha Lloyd, who quilted with her sisters, never married. Highly respected and loved, she never moved from the cottage at Colston until the day she died. After a long life, Martha's funeral was held as the Second World War was raging. Martha, herself, was devoted to the Prince of Peace – and her home! Daily chores were a pleasure and privilege for this beautiful woman who took pride in all the ordinary tasks. She swept the floor with her brush, collected the eggs that were warm from the hens and stored them until they were ready to be cooked or sold. It was Martha who carefully poured milk into the saucepan and watched over it until it came to the boil, sterilised and safe for the family to drink.

Martha's greatest love, though, was for her Lord and she was there without fail at Beulah Chapel for every meeting. The sound of her clogs announced her entrance as she went to her seat close to her sister, Ann, and brother-in-law, James. After a brief smile of acknowledgment, Martha bowed her head to pray. All the men in the area saw her devotion and loved her for her pure nature and, after her death, Willie Adams, a local agricultural labourer who worked at Martel Farm, spoke for many when he wrote a poem about Martha after visiting her grave in the grounds of Beulah. The poem was published in the *County Echo* in 1944.

Deigryn Galar ar Fedd y Diweddar Martha Lloyd, Golstwn, Castellnewydd Bach

Mae angau yn talu ymweliad
Yn amal a'r ardal ers tro:
Yn cipio i ffwrdd ein rhai annwyl
Yn ddistaw i arall fro;
Yn ei dro daeth i bentref y Golstwn
A chipiodd i ffwrdd Martha Lloyd,
Cym'doges a Sant o'r fath oreu

A welodd yr ardal erioed.

Ti aethost gan adael dy ffrindiau
Mewn acen hiraethus eu iaith,
A'r oll o'th gym'dogion sydd heddyw
A'u llygaid a'u gruddiau yn llaith;
A briw ddaeth i'm calon pa ddiwrnod
Wrth weled beth barodd i'm chwith,
Sef canfod dieithriaid dideimlad
Yn brysur yn chwalu dy nyth.

Ti dreuliaist oes gyfan i'w bluo,
Edrychai bob amser yn hardd:
'Roedd son drwy yr ardal mor gymen
Y cedrwydd y bwthyn a'r ardd:
Yn fuan bydd chwyn yn ymsythu,
Yr ysgall a'r hen ddant-y-llew,
A'r bwthyn yn cael ei falurio
Gan wyntoedd a chenllysg rhew.

Fel Martha gynt draw ym Methania,
Trafferthion y ty aeth a'th fryd
Canys hwnnw a'r Capel yn Beulah
Oeddynt bopeth i ti yn y byd:
'Mhob oedfa boed tywydd a fynno
Yn brydlon oet ti yn dy sedd,
Parheaist ar hyd y blynyddoedd
Yn ffyddlon o'th grud hyd dy fedd.

'Wyt heddyw yn nghwmni dy Geidwad
A geraist mor fawr drwy dy oes,
Yn canu yn mhlith dy hoff geraint
Am rinwedd rhyfeddol y Groes:
Dwed wrth y rhai gwrddi di yno

Mae disgwyl yr alwad 'rym ni
Yn fuan bydd rhagor o'th ffrindiau
Yn nofio'r Iorddonen a'i lli.

Gobeithio cawn eto rhyw ddiwrnod
Dy gwrdd ar y 'lan brydferth draw',
'Rwyn siwr os cei gyfle mi fyddi
'Da'r cyntaf i estyn dy law
'Rol gorphen holl 'daith yr anialwch'
Mewn gwlad sydd heb gystudd na phoen,
Cawn yno cydorphwys a gwledda
Ar gariad arhraethol yr Oen.

W.S. Adams

A Tear of Grief at the Grave of the Late Martha Lloyd, Colston, Little Newcastle.

(a rough translation)

For some time, death has been
Paying a visit to the district,
Silently snatching away to other pastures,
Some of our dear ones.
It came in its turn to Colston Village
And snatched away Martha Lloyd,
The best kind of neighbour and saint
That the district has ever seen.

You departed, leaving your friends
With longing in their voice:
Today, all of your neighbours
Have moist eyes and cheeks.
What was sad to me was to behold
The strange feeling of seeing how

Quickly your nest had been scattered.
You spent your life feathering it
It always looked so beautiful
People around spoke of the order there was
In the cottage; its cedarwood and garden.
Soon there'll be the boastful cry
Of the thorn and the dandelion
And the cottage will crumble
With the winds and the freezing hail.

Like Martha before you in Bethany,
The cares of the house were in your nature
Because that and the chapel in Beulah
Were all the world to you.
Whatever the weather, you were there
On time for every Meeting;
You carried on throughout the years,
Faithful from the cradle to the grave.

Today, you're in the company of the Saviour
Whom you loved so much in life,
Singing with your beloved family
Of the wonderful virtues of the Cross.
Tell some of those you meet there
That we're expecting the call.
Soon there'll be more of your friends
Swimming on the tide of Jordan.

I hope that we'll meet again some day
In the beautiful, sacred place beyond.
If you get the chance, I'm sure that you'll
Be the first to stretch out your hand to me
When the wilderness journey is over

In a kingdom without affliction or pain.
We'll be able to rest together and feast
On the abundant love of the Lamb.

Martha Lloyd had no more need of the earthly cottage that she had loved and tended. The home where Samuel and Mary Lloyd had lived, the home that their children had known, the home that Martha had never left, was finally to change hands. On January 20th, 1944, the *County Echo* advised its readers of the Sale by Auction of Colston cottage and its contents.

The stone-built Colston Cottage with its living room, bedroom and workroom, its garden, coalhouse and pigsty was up for sale to be enjoyed by another family. Other people bought the old Welsh dresser, the armchairs, dining chairs and children's chairs – all made from antique oak. The settles, kitchen table, round table and side tables, press, cupboard bed and wooden bed, changed hands. So did a wall clock, feather bed with pillows and bolsters, Willow pattern dishes and plates, antique jugs and mugs, ornaments, pictures, kettles, saucepans, garden tools, pig trough and ladder. An era was over.

Samuel and Mary Lloyd's four sons, Thomas, William, John and James (Martha's brothers), were born at a time when rural living was becoming increasingly difficult for those who owned no land. Little is known or remembered of three of these sons born to Samuel and Mary. As an adolescent, Thomas became a carpenter like his father but then in manhood, he disappeared like his brothers, John and James. Did they succumb to disease prematurely, did they move right away from the area in search of a better life? Did they lose their lives in some battle? Some questions remain unanswered because life is not that neat and orderly – but what became of their other son, William?

WILLIAM LLOYD
at Little Newcastle and Letterston

William Lloyd was born in 1853 and his responsibilities began when he was a young boy. Like his brothers and sisters, he was helping in small ways and doing anything he could to bring a few pennies home. William worked on the land and soon learnt to respect it and the animals in his charge. He was another lad who would continue the tradition of agricultural labouring.

He knew that it would be hard and strenuous work and didn't expect it to be anything else. The energy needed for the labour always built up his appetite and he was certainly ready for his food! His mother, Mary, gave him tea and bread at six in the morning before he began work – and that kept him going until bread and cheese was brought out to him and the others in the field at about ten o'clock. He put his spade down for a few minutes as he bit into the delicious, salty cheese before swallowing it down. Then it was back to work until mid-day when the main meal was brought out to all the men. On a chilly day, there was nothing as good as the bowl of *cawl* that came fresh from the pot – the chewy lamb and the soft vegetables, each with their own distinctive taste, helped to fill his stomach. Sometimes, he found little suet dumplings in the broth, which was better still! He was refreshed enough to dig a little deeper into the ground until another break came when he saw one of the girls bringing tea and bread out at four in the afternoon. Then, at the end of the day, when he was tired and work was finally over, it was back to Colston cottage for a supper of bread, milk and a little oatmeal. The salted bacon hanging in the kitchen made his mouth water and his mother gave him extra treats when she could – he was still a growing boy, after all!

There was less work to do on the farms in the winter so everyone was able to take a break from the usual routine to enjoy the Christmas festivities. Apart from Christmas itself, New Year's

Day was also a lot of fun. William got up early before the sun had risen and took a bowl from the cottage before meeting up with his friends and cousins outside. They had no time to waste as they scrambled up to reach the well before anyone else. Once they'd reached the running water, the bowl was placed underneath so that they could catch plenty of it. It was freezing cold but that didn't trouble the boys. All they cared about was having a good supply in the bowl for, as this was the first water of the year to be collected, it brought good fortune. Lots of people said that this was healing, holy water too – so the lads were welcomed when they took it around to the houses. Sometimes, on their way, they saw a neighbour on the road and the sprig of holly was firmly dipped in the bowl as they made sure that the passing friend was sprinkled with the holy water. There was lots of laughter and banter as the boys were given a coin for their efforts. Then, they set off for the houses. After a sharp knock on the door, William and the other boys sang as loudly as they could:

"O, Dyma'r Flwyddyn Newydd,

O, Dyma'r Flwyddyn Newydd,

O, Dyma'r Flwyddyn Newydd,

Llawenydd trwy bob lle"

(O, here comes the New Year, Happiness to every place!)

When the door was opened, they went inside, carried on with their singing and sprinkled every room in the house as well as the people! William loved this custom and no-one turned them away without a penny in their pockets or a bite to eat. What happier way could there be to begin another year? Everyone needed to believe that good fortune was on its way and the few coppers went a long way in the leaner winter months.

Catherine Morgan lived in the nearby village of Letterston. Two miles was no distance at all at hay-making time or when potatoes were lifted and, as he grew a little older, William sensed an attraction to this young girl. Catherine was the daughter of another agricultural labourer and her family had never moved from Letterston. There wasn't a great deal of free time for the young couple to meet up very much, but, after a long courtship, they decided that they wanted to marry.

Once they were sure about this, they had to go through the customary rituals. First of all, William had to tell his father, Samuel, of his intention. He was nervous about this but he had worried in vain because his father raised no objections. Samuel's next task was to go down to Letterston to speak to Catherine's father, Henry Morgan. Again, the couple had an anxious wait but the news was good – Henry was happy about the wedding, too! Samuel began making arrangements for William and Catherine to live in a little leased cottage in Letterston and invitations to the wedding were sent out – no-one in Letterston or Little Newcastle would be left out!

Although the Penny Post had been available for thirty years, the people of North Pembrokeshire were slow to use it and preferred to rely on the ancient custom of 'bidding'. A 'bidder' (*gwahoddwr*) was called in, given his instructions and then sent out to every household to tell them about the forthcoming marriage. Catherine Morgan and William Lloyd were to be wed in St. Giles' Church, Letterston, on a February day in 1876. All the guests began to think of a gift for the young couple and people with special skills started to make presents – the couple were fortunate to have a carpenter in the family as well as William's sisters who made beautiful quilts. However, most of the guests decided to bring presents of money. For a couple such as William and Catherine, who *had* very little and were unlikely to have much in the future from labouring alone, these gifts were very gratefully received. The princely sum of thirty pounds was a great asset as they began their married life – full of hope for the future and happy in the knowledge that they had their loving families around them for support. William's people were at hand in Little Newcastle and Catherine's relatives, the Morgan and the Davies families, were even closer.

HENRY and ELIZABETH MORGAN, JOHN and ANN DAVIES in Letterston

John and Ann Davies were spending the winter evening in Henry and Elizabeth Morgan's cottage. Knitting stockings and making baskets were good ways of passing the dark hours after supper before tiredness overcame them. In spite of their advanced years, the two men still worked as agricultural labourers and their wives helped out in the farmhouse kitchen or in the fields at busy times of the year. The Vicar had told them the year of their births once – he said that Henry and Elizabeth were born in 1776, John in 1769 and Ann in 1761 – but years written down like that didn't mean a lot to them. It was easier to remember their lives by the harvests, the harsh winters or the birth of their children.

Knitting and basket-making brought them a small income but these evenings gave them a chance to chat and enjoy each others' company too. There was plenty to talk about as both couples knew every inch of this little patch of inland Pembrokeshire between Haverfordwest and Fishguard – and every inhabitant!

Elizabeth and Margaret listened to their husbands' chatting in Welsh as they continued clicking their needles in an effort to finish another stocking before the rush-light faded. Their fingers knew the patterns even in the darkness but they needed a bit of light to change a ball of wool or turn the needles tidily at the heel.

They had all seen so many changes!

"Who'd have thought that we'd live to see the day when a Church came to be built here, Henry bach!" mused John, "and that Vicarage as big as any farm, with its schoolroom, servants' quarters and corn loft – not to mention the living rooms for the Minister's family."

"Aye!" replied Henry, nodding his head in agreement. The two women smiled at each other briefly. Reminiscing always kept their men talking.

"And Saron chapel, too!"

"And now a school!"

"Aye!"

The two men fell silent for a moment, concentrating on their work and reflecting on how different life was now. Henry glanced over to check that the fire was doing well and reckoned that there was still a bit of time left on the rush-light.

"*We* never had any schooling" muttered John, as if to himself. "And neither did our children. Not that it did us any harm. What good is learning when you're out in the fields?"

Henry thought about this, before adding, "It might help our young ones – our great-grandchildren – to get out of this life and find something better. We know how hard it's been, John, crammed in together, never knowing if the farmers will keep us on and, God knows, we've seen some harvests fail! Perhaps they'll be able to make new starts with a bit of schooling and not suffer like we have done over the years…"

John was not convinced. "You need money and land to make a break, Henry," he said. "Learning alone will do nothing for them."

The men were quiet again, each silently wondering how the future would be for the babies and children in their families.

The burnt-down rush-light had crackled to its end and the air was thick with its smoke. Anne finished her row of stitches and put the knitting in a little bag. She stood up and wished Elizabeth good-night as the two men began to stir. They were all ready for bed but John hesitated for a moment at Henry and Elizabeth's doorway. He was puzzled. "Is it turnips in the top field, this year, Henry?"

Henry frowned. "Turnips...um....turnips?" It was hard to remember the order of the crops sometimes but he had a feeling that turnips had just been. "No, it's not *turnips*," he said, still mystified. "*Oats*? Is it *oats*?" Again, he hesitated. Surely they had oats the year before the turnips in the top field? "No, it's not oats" he mused. Suddenly, the answer came to him and he was pleased with himself as he replied. "No, it's not oats or turnips" he said, "It's *clover!*"

"*Clover!* Of course!" John smiled, glad that the matter was settled. It would soon be time to get the earth ready again; there was no frost that night.

John and Anne left for their own cottage and Elizabeth, seeing that Henry was attending to the fire, put her knitting away and went up to bed.

On his own, Henry poked the fire carefully and considered where to place the culm. Like the other labourers, Henry had been allowed to take some of the clay from the land belonging to the Vicarage so that he could mix it with coal dust and add water to make it up into a paste. Once the paste had been made, he'd moulded it in his hands to form little balls about the size of an egg from a good, healthy hen. This was the precious culm! A few balls, well-placed on the night fire, burned slowly and ensured that the fire was still in when they woke in the morning.

Satisfied that the fire was taken care of, Henry made his own way to bed. He knew that it would soon be his time to move on to God's garden. Maybe he'd be able to enjoy the land then instead of labouring on it! But the work was so much part of him that he wouldn't be able to stop himself! He thought about his children and his grandchildren and was grateful for them all. It had been a good evening with John and Anne, he thought.

They enjoyed each others' company and they shared some grandchildren. John and Anne's daughter, Margaret, had married Henry and Elizabeth's son – another Henry Morgan. He hoped that life would be kind to them all.

Gweddi Henry Morgan

D'oes dim arian gen i ar y ddaear,
Trugarha wrth ddyn syml fel myfi.
D'oes dim tir gen i ar y ddaear,
Trugarha wrth ddyn syml fel myfi.
D'oes dim byd gen i ar y ddaear,
Trugarha wrth ddyn syml fel myfi.
D'oedd dim arian gen Ti ar y ddaear,
Trugarha wrth ddyn syml fel myfi.
D'oedd dim tir gen Ti ar y ddaear,
Trugarha wrth ddyn syml fel myfi.
D'oedd dim byd gen Ti ar y ddaear,
Trugarha wrth ddyn syml fel myfi.

Henry Morgan's Prayer

I have no money on the earth
Have mercy on a simple man like me.
I have no land on the earth,
Have mercy on a simple man like me.
I have no possessions on the earth,
Have mercy on a simple man like me.
You had no money on the earth,
Have mercy on a simple man like me.
You had no land on the earth,
Have mercy on a simple man like me.
You had no possessions on the earth,
Have mercy on a simple man like me.

HENRY MORGAN and MARGARET DAVIES
at Letterston

Henry Morgan stood at the open doorway of the labourer's cottage that was his home. He didn't often have the time to stand and stare but his daughter, Catherine, was attending to her hair before marrying William Lloyd. These preparations were things for the women to fuss about and there was no room in the cottage for privacy so he turned his eyes outwards.

He found himself wondering about the sort of life the young couple would have together. The Lloyd family from Little Newcastle were good, respected people but William was only an agricultural labourer. Henry knew all about the hardships of the job because he, too, was an agricultural labourer. He couldn't read or write but he knew how to use the plough, he had strong hands and arms for digging and he understood the animals. William and Catherine would have the same long working hours, their cottage would be crammed full once the children started arriving, they'd be at the mercy of the farmers and the moods of the seasons; there'd be times when the wells would dry up and they'd have long treks to get any water. Catherine was not the first of his children to marry – she was the seventh of their brood. His wife, Margaret, had brought her into the world as an early Christmas gift back in 1849. It didn't seem so long ago! In spite of the hardships, he and Margaret had managed – so there was no reason why this young couple shouldn't do the same. And what was the point of worrying, anyhow?

Henry heard the giggling inside so he knew that Catherine was still not ready. What was it about women that took them so long? It *was* her wedding-day so he left them to their affairs. On this early spring day, he breathed in the fresh, country air that was already losing its chill. He saw the new turnpike road ahead of him that linked Haverfordwest to Fishguard and, for a moment,

Henry allowed himself a satisfied smile. *He* had been one of the men to build that little bit of the road and he was proud of his achievement. Bad roads had always been a problem years ago and, though everyone agreed that new ones were needed, there had been riots when the tolls came to pay for them. It had been the same old story of the poor people being pushed into an impossible situation. Landowners could afford to pay the tolls without any problem but the small farmers struggled – and it was even worse for labourers like himself who had to pay just for carting lime to improve the soil. Henry smiled again as he remembered how it had all happened. Even though they spread to other parts of West and South Wales, the Rebecca Riots had started here in Pembrokeshire!

Thomas Rees, from Mynachlog-ddu, had the idea first – yes, it all came flooding back to Henry now! Thomas and his friends had burned down the toll gates and they attacked them again when they were re-built. They'd dressed up as women to disguise themselves and they wouldn't give in, even when the troops were called in. The news even got into the London papers and lots of important people up in the English city sympathised with them – the ordinary people!

Charges had been made fairer so the battle had not been in vain. When it was time for the turnpike road to be built in Letterston, local men were asked to do the work on the stretch of their own native village. The farmers had to release some of their labourers to do the job and Henry was chosen. He was about sixty at the time, it was a dusty old job and even harder on the back and legs than working on the land – but it brought him better wages for a few years and he was grateful for that. He had seven daughters, after all!

Henry peered inside the cottage briefly again and it looked as if Catherine was almost ready – but they were fussing about some flowers. The cottage was still filled with women's business so he left them to it.

All the Letterston folk were gathering outside to catch a glimpse of them and Henry felt proud of these people whom he knew so well. They had all seen so many changes here in the village and, when he was born in 1816, things had been very different! Now, with the new road, who knew what the future would hold? At last, Henry heard Catherine's footsteps coming towards him and he turned round to see his daughter looking very beautiful. As they left the cottage to make their way down to the church, he was proud to have her on his arm, knowing that she would make a good wife for William Lloyd. All he could do now was to hope and pray that their lives would be blessed with children and good fortune.

WILLIAM LLOYD and CATHERINE MORGAN at Letterston

As William and Catherine Lloyd set their wedding gifts aside, they had no idea that they would need to rely on them so quickly. Within months of their marriage, William came to the conclusion that most of his efforts that year had been in vain. He reaped in a very poor harvest. Everybody else had a similar tale to tell and the spirits of the whole farming community sank. 1876 had brought one of the worst harvests within living memory. Prices had to rise on all the goods that were being sent down to the industrial South by train. The big land-owners could keep back a portion of their own crops with no problem but the small farmers fared worse. As usual, it was the poor who suffered most and the plight of the agricultural labourers was dire. The failed yield came at a time when so many were losing their jobs anyway because of the modern tools and equipment. William and Catherine wondered how they would survive.

Local people were desperate to find food and everyone was out scavenging for the food in the fields. Nettles were gathered to make good, nourishing soups, dandelions were pulled up by the handful so that hot drinks could be made by roasting the roots; the bitter leaves provided a salad that kept them strong. There was a scramble to get to the blackberry bushes but they, too, were soon bare of their fruits. William and Catherine were more fortunate than many because of their large, local families. Admittedly, there were more mouths to feed but everyone was prepared to share what they had and keep up the morale.

Many of the country people who had resisted moving, finally decided to get on the trains and go South to find work – others sailed off to America. Hunger doesn't offer great choices. In spite of the difficulties, William and Catherine stayed put in Letterston. Catherine had felt the movement of her first baby inside her. This was no time to move away. Little Samuel was born just months after the disastrous harvest and he helped his parents focus on the present and believe in the future. William and Catherine struggled on and more children were born – Mary, Elizabeth (Eliza), Henry and Jane. In 1901, a further blow hit them all when another miserable harvest questioned their chances of remaining in the country.

Another century had just begun but the situation was no better. If anything, it was worse and, for the first time ever, there was no work for William, Catherine and their family in Letterston. They wondered if they'd be forced to move away from Pembrokeshire this time but they were respected, conscientious workers and a farmer in Maenclochog took them on. Grateful for any employment, they made the journey to the new village at the foothills of the Preselis. Here, at Rhydfach, William and Catherine worked unstintingly and, when another baby arrived, Catherine just carried on with her tasks with the little one wrapped around her in a shawl. They were determined to prove their worth. Life is never predictable and there was an even greater disaster to face. William Lloyd, head of the family and father of five, died. The children now had to support their widowed mother, Catherine.

The boys were freer than the girls to leave and make their own lives. Henry left Pembrokeshire altogether for Liverpool. People said that the cities were paved with gold and he decided to test this out for himself. Elizabeth (Eliza) stayed on at Rhydfach until she eventually married and, even then, she only returned to her native village of Letterston.

The children of WILLIAM and CATHERINE LLOYD

Elizabeth (Eliza) Lewis (née Lloyd)

Eliza and her husband had a tiny cottage in Letterston on the edge of the road that led to St. David's. It was from here that Eliza had their five children – William John (Willie), Tom, Jane, Luke and Kate. Life wasn't getting any easier in the country though the goods that arrived with the trains had brought a few shops to the village and some general commerce. Even this improvement brought limited advantages for, shortly after the birth of their youngest child, the First World War was declared. Eliza's husband survived the battle only to die of influenza in the Spanish 'Flu Epidemic of 1918.

How would Eliza manage now? She had to use any skills she had and her working childhood served her well. Eliza made rush-mats. These rushes were gathered in the summer and dried before Eliza could use them. She laid the rushes down on the floor, side by side then plaited the first three rushes together, then another three and another three... When she had enough plaits, she lined them up on the floor so that they were level with each other and then sewed them together before stitching the ends so that they wouldn't fray. They were popular and the welcoming rush-mat on the stone step of her own front-door, remained there until it was worn. When it was eventually too delicate to repair, it was time for Eliza to make a new one. Somehow, she managed and the children grew up.

Willie stayed in Letterston, married, had children and worked with horses. He was well-known for his expertise with the animals and, if anyone had an equestrian problem, Willie was the man to sort it out. One day, a horse in his care became nervous and even Willie was unable to calm it. He was trampled to death. His widow took in washing.

Tom moved to Camrose (a small village nearby) and became a lay-preacher in the Baptist Chapel. His strict Nonconformist ideals didn't prevent him from enjoying the latest trends in men's fashions – he was quite a dandy.

Kate stayed in Pembrokeshire and became a farmer's wife.

I remember Auntie Eliza and two of her children well.

Auntie Eliza was very much like my other aunts in the country. She lived in a small white-washed cottage that looked pretty on the outside, especially when the sun shone and made the walls shiny like whipped egg-white. But, inside, there was hardly any light coming in at all through the few small windows.

She was tiny and pale with a thin, white face that looked so sad. She wore black clothes that seemed to cover all her body apart from the tense little face and hands. Auntie Eliza never smiled.

When my mother and I called to see her, Auntie Eliza made a cup of tea and offered us a biscuit before sitting down in the darkest corner of the room herself. When she did this, her clothes faded into the background so that all I could see was the tired, old face staring out at me and white hands with big, blue veins.

She and my mother talked about things I didn't understand and about people I didn't know so I didn't really concentrate. However, there was one conversation that I remember very clearly.

Auntie Eliza looked, if anything, sadder than usual, when she asked my mother a question. She said the words slowly. "Harry never loved that other woman, did he?"

This was obviously a serious question and I wondered what was going to happen. My mother was a very emotional woman and she often cried. Was she going to cry now? I never knew what to do when she burst into tears. The silence seemed to be very long. I could hear my heart beating.

My mother took her time to reply but, when she did speak, her voice was clear and even. She shook her head and said "He turned to her in his grief."

I looked up at both of them. Auntie Eliza's face was a bit softer. Her lips were almost smiling.

Luke and Jane were two of Auntie Eliza's children. I remember them and their families well.

Luke Lewis

Luke was a thin, delicate-looking man with no colour in his face at all. He was another person who had a sad smile and was totally different from his wife, Maggie. Maggie had been born and brought up in Llanwnda where, as a young girl, she was used to getting up at half-past four in the morning, slipping her feet into clogs and going out to turn the hay with her pitchfork. Well-rounded, rosy-cheeked, cheerful and chatty, she and Luke made an interesting couple. Luke worked as a shunter with the trains down in Fishguard Harbour and returned every night to their little cottage in Llanwnda. It was made out of corrugated tin and seemed like something from a fairy-tale, where, if you huffed and puffed, and you huffed and puffed, you might blow it down. But it was stronger than it looked and stood firm in its exposed position against a headland crag. The view from the cottage was stunning and, wherever you looked, there was the temperamental sea below with seals jumping out to play and birds flying around with their noisy cries, always searching for a tit-bit and swooping down to capture it. We had to climb the steep hill from Goodwick and then walk an extra mile or two to get to this fascinating place but, oddly enough, I never remember being tired.

I used to play with Luke and Maggie's two daughters and we had a lot of fun running around outside with the salt wind blowing on our faces. Everything was fine until I needed to use the toilet. People used different words for this place and I never knew the right one. 'Lavatory' was thought to be vulgar but the new expressions of 'resting-room' or the 'powder room' seemed out-of-place. It was as if everyone was ashamed of this little room that we all needed and I'd picked up the embarrassment. So I went up to my mother and whispered my need to her. She then whispered the news to Maggie who beamed and asked the girls to show me the way.

I was used to outside toilets (my paternal grandparents had one) but this particular one was a long walk right down the garden. I was shown the place and, as I looked inside, I saw some earth with a plank of wood on top of it. The wood had two round holes and there was no sign of a chain.

A little miracle happened – I didn't want to go anymore!

Jane George (née Lewis)

Jane was Auntie Eliza's daughter and she lived with her husband and son on the other side of the road from her mother. The house was quite big and its front-room was Jane's shop. The shop was the entrance to the house, so whenever we called to see Jane, we had to pass through it first – it was like Aladdin's cave! There was paint and string, pegs and cards, china and writing-pads… (I still have a tray from Jane's shop).

Jane and my mother got on very well so, after yet another cup of tea, the two of them chatted away happily and quickly to make up for lost time. They didn't get the chance to meet often. Jane was an outstandingly beautiful woman – elegant and serene with a lovely smile that seemed to permanently grace her face. One day, my mother asked her for the secret of her flawless skin.

Jane stood up. "Come!" she beckoned and we followed her upstairs to the bedroom. We sat on the bed as she walked over to her dressing-table and reached for a little glass bottle with some pink liquid inside. She unscrewed the top of the bottle and smiled as she smelt its contents. "Come!" she said to my mother and held out her hand so that my mother gave her hand with upturned wrists to touch Jane's. Then, with that smile that made her seem like a queen or a princess, Jane held my mother's hand as she poured a little of the liquid onto her wrists. "Rub it in!" she said, still smiling. My mother rubbed it in, round and round, until it disappeared miraculously. Then, Jane told her to lift her wrist to her nose. The two cousins smiled at each other and sighed with pleasure. Jane saw that I was interested too so she asked for my hand and I offered it to her with my wrist upturned. A little drop of pink milk fell onto my skin and I rubbed it round and round until it disappeared. I lifted my wrist to my nose and smiled. Jane's face was beaming. "See!" she said, simply.

I looked at the bottle and read the words 'Oil of Ulay'. It all sounded very exotic – the sort of thing I expected from someone who kept a shop that was like Aladdin's cave. I'd only heard of olive oil before and 'Ulay' sounded foreign.

I've had a soft spot for Oil of Ulay ever since!

Jane was a popular family name that had been used through the generations. Jane with her 'Oil of Ulay' could remember her mother's sister who had been another Jane.

Jane Lloyd at Maenclochog

Jane Lloyd was born in 1887 and moved around with her parents and siblings as they found work in various cottages in different parts of Letterston. She was sixteen when they all moved away to Rhydfach cottage in Maenclochog. This beautiful young woman remained in the isolated village for a further ten years, working on the farm and helping out at home. Things became very difficult when her father, William, died and she had a duty to help her widowed mother.

Jane knew that there was the hope of a better life ahead but she had to be patient! For some time, she had been receiving letters from Henry Griffiths of Llanwnda – and she treasured them. Written carefully and elegantly by hand, they were a source of great comfort to her when time seemed to be passing her by. Jane and her sisters had to ensure that all was well for their mother. Henry – Harry – wanted her hand in marriage but he had vowed to wait until he could offer Jane the security of a decent home. Only then would he return to marry her.

HENRY and JANE GRIFFITHS at Abercynon

At last, the wedding between the two lovers took place in Horeb Baptist Chapel, Maenclochog on a winter's day, early in 1914. The families enjoyed a meal together before Harry proudly took the new Mrs. Griffiths to Abercynon. He knew it would be a shock as she had never left the little Pembrokeshire villages before – but he promised that he'd always protect her. After all, he had just pledged to cherish and honour her before his God and all their relatives. That was exactly what he was determined to do.

Abercynon in Glamorganshire had been a place of little significance to anyone but the handful of farmers and labourers who lived there in the early eighteenth-century. They knew their little corner of Wales well with its mountains, long valleys and rushing rivers. It was here that the Rivers Cynon and Taff joined forces to swell their waters that ran down to the sea at Cardiff. Everything had changed with the coming of the 'black diamonds'! Coal had to be transported from the pits so The Glamorganshire Canal had come in 1795 and then the Taff Vale Railway arrived in the 1840s. Hundreds of men were needed to mine this coal and they were needed quickly to meet the increasing demand. The valley seemed to change overnight as hasty efforts were made to build homes for all these workers. Rows and rows of little terraced houses were constructed quickly, back-to-back, on all the flat land – and then more spilled out up onto the hillsides as more men arrived. They came from the Welsh countryside to find work but, as word spread about the scale of the industry, others arrived from England. Churches and chapels sprang up, schools were opened for all the children as the little hamlet now had to cater for the three thousand men who worked here, producing half a million tons of coal every year.

This was the Abercynon that Jane Griffiths saw. Even on the biggest farm in the busiest season, there had been nothing like this. There were so many people everywhere – and more houses crammed into a valley than she had seen in her entire life. Harry showed her to the rooms he had rented and was happy that their new life would finally free them from the poverty they had endured in Pembrokeshire.

Harry had already had time to adapt to everything, of course, and he was patient as Jane learnt to accept her new environment. It wasn't easy for her to be at home every day on her own while Harry was working underground in a place that she couldn't even begin to imagine. Fortunately, there was a great community spirit in Abercynon and she soon befriended the neighbours who all shared the same experience of a life governed by coal. These bonds helped to compensate for the yearning she had for her family back in Pembrokeshire.

Just as she and Harry were settling down, War was declared. At first, there was general support for it and there was certainly no problem in getting men to sign up. Britain had so many allies as well as the strength of the British Empire. It would all be over by Christmas and peace would be restored. The war effort needed all the coal it could get – so Harry's job as a miner was an important one. Christmas came but there was no sign of an end to the hostilities. On the contrary, everyone was hearing about huge numbers of casualties and, day after day, week after week, somebody seemed to have bad news of a loved one.

Mining was no easy option to fighting and Harry was injured underground although the damage was not too extensive. By the end of 1914, Jane gave birth to their first child. Their joy was muted as the War was still claiming so many lives but Harry and Jane were pleased with their little daughter and gave her an impressive string of names. She was to be called Peggy Gwenllian Lloyd Griffiths.

1915 came. 1916 came – and still there was no sign of the War ending. So many men had lost their lives by this time that there was talk of conscripting men. If this happened, Harry and his colleagues would be exempt because of their job. This war was very dependent on the coal industry. The War wouldn't go on for ever and Harry had a dream. He was gregarious and got on well with all sorts of people; he was not afraid of hard-work and he had an eye for opportunity. He wanted to start a little business. But how could this happen? He reckoned that, if he was careful with money, he could rent a shop. The family could live above the shop and he would be able to work there when he had finished his shift underground. If the venture succeeded, he might be able to buy it eventually. Peace would come one day.

A shop became available in Margaret Street – the main commercial street in Abercynon. Harry and Jane went down to look at it and they were excited at what they saw. Downstairs, there was a big front-room where the goods for sale could be displayed and the back room downstairs could be the store-room for the rest of the stock. On the first floor, there were several rooms, and this would be their family home. As if this weren't enough, there was a little attic room on the top floor where the children could play. It was ideal. Harry boldly agreed to take it on and he moved in with Jane and little Peggy. After his working-day was over, Harry began to order stock. The town needed a china shop with other useful, household goods to bring in extra customers. His prices would be fair because the least these men and their families deserved was honesty.

Harry and Jane set to work. Goods were ordered and displayed; the account-book was ready and the shop was open! Of course the hours were difficult but, compared with so many others, life was being kind to them. They were happy when Jane gave birth to another little daughter in 1916 and, again, the couple enjoyed the process of choosing the names. Catherine Mildred Morgan Griffiths was an impressive title for a little baby! Sadly, she only lived for ten days. The War was still killing thousands, women were used to losing some of their babies but, nevertheless, every death carried its own, unique pain. Neighbours rallied round the couple, offering them the love that they, themselves, always gave out so generously to others. The baby was buried up in the local hillside cemetery and, though they knew she was no more physically, it was comforting to have a grave where they could lay flowers.

Peggy was now delighting her parents as she began to walk and talk and Harry and Jane had their whole life before them. Nothing would bring little Catherine back and life had to go on! There was still no sign of an end to the War. In that same year, thousands of British men had been killed in the Battle of the Somme alone and the mood in the country was changing as no-one had expected such terrible losses. Harry was always discussing it at work and Jane worried about it with her neighbours. Could War ever be justified? The Government had asked Ministers in churches and chapels to preach about this 'just war' that was confronting a greater evil. Some of them toed the line but others refused to advocate fighting from the pulpit. What was the right thing to do? They were all asking the same question! And when would there be some peace?

Harry continued working underground every day and he

returned to attend to the shop. His wages were helping him to finance the business and, before long, he hoped that he'd be able to buy it. It was certainly doing very well. Maybe, one day...?

In 1918, there was cause for great celebration when the War finally ended. Most families had lost loved ones but, at last, there was to be peace in the country. However, in the same year, another scourge affected families across the world and killed more people than the War itself. As if people hadn't suffered enough, an epidemic of Spanish 'Flu broke out. There was more loss and pain for millions of families who couldn't believe that a new disaster had hit so hard immediately after a devastating War. The Griffiths family were so grateful that they had been spared from these tragedies. Yes, they had lost one little baby and Harry's accident at work had given him permanent scars on his face and hands – but they had not known the terrible experiences they'd heard about in the rat-infested trenches; they had survived the 'Flu epidemic. Harry was employed, they had little Peggy and good living accommodation.

As a woman who had just turned thirty, Jane was now eligible to vote for the first time and she looked forward to going to the booth to have her say in the political situation in the country. Peace had been restored and she wanted it to stay that way so that people could just return to their ordinary lives. In the following year, she gave birth to another daughter and, again, the baby was generously endowed with names. This little girl was Phoebe Ann Henner Griffiths but, after all the effort of the naming, no-one called her anything other than Nancy. Nancy was a healthy baby and, it was only when she failed to walk at the usual time that her parents realised that she had some sort of a problem. But she was a happy little child and these things often sorted themselves out in time.

The family knew that they had been well-blessed. Jane loved the feel of silk – especially shantung silk – that delicate fabric that has to be ironed when it's bone dry. Harry bought silk dresses for Jane and they made an elegant couple as they went down to chapel with their immaculately-dressed children. Harry was now in a position to buy the shop and a couple of others in the Valley. He finally left his mining job as he took this bold step forward and reckoned that, as he'd use the same stock to supply all the shops, he just needed to place a larger order, get it delivered and find someone to manage the other shops for him. Everyone was eager to find jobs after the War. Harry bought a motor-car so that it was easier to collect the stock and take it from shop to shop. There weren't many cars in Abercynon at the time and everybody waved at the Griffiths family as they passed by. Harry and Jane were a popular couple. Harry was loved for his integrity, fairness, the twinkle in his eye and a sense of humour. Jane was respected for her kind, loving ways – and everyone was attracted by her beauty.

Delighted as they were with their two daughters, there was great excitement when Jane gave birth to a son. Again, the baby bore a host of family names; William Benjamin Owen Griffiths was their healthy son and heir. Harry and Jane were still very much in love and their family life was very precious to them. They smiled as they watched the children having fun with a little china tea-set upstairs in the attic-room. In their wildest dreams, they had not expected such good fortune. When another daughter arrived in 1923, they were delighted and, as was their custom, they gave the new baby an impressive collection of names. Nesta May Georgina Griffiths was the new addition to the family.

Jane felt unwell one day as she was feeding little Nesta but she carried on working. It was difficult to sit down and rest with a young family. Harry eventually insisted that she went to bed. Jane had a fever but felt shivery at the same time. Harry called on his close friends to take the children away and he looked after Jane himself, applying cold compresses with the tenderness of a woman. He waited for Jane to reach the turning-point – the 'crisis'. It didn't come. Jane had contracted influenza which developed into pneumonia. Three days earlier, Jane had been a young, healthy nursing mother. Now, she was dead.

Harry was distraught. How could his beloved, darling Jane have left him so quickly? He had cared for her with such devotion! He adored her! As he stayed alone with her, he refused to let go of his beautiful wife for a while. He wept as he lifted her head and combed her long, dark hair. When it was shining, he parted and plaited it. Heart-broken, his next task was to tell the children.

The Home Above The Shop

The motherless children huddle, motherless,
In the happy home above the shop.
A handful of lives now sustained
Alone by a father's grieving gaze.

First motherless child. A girl.
Seeking the breasts now drained of milk and life,
Six months on from enclosed womb
This baby's needs in enclosed tomb.

Second motherless child. A boy.
Too young to know, words a babble.
No comfort from another robs
This waif of his pleading, needy sobs.

Third motherless child. A girl.
She cannot walk; a twisted spine.
A lift to kiss the face in peace
Her Mam loaned, too short a lease.

Fourth motherless child. A girl.
Earthly feelings, shadows unknown.

In death she found her mother's arms,
Discovered joy in spirit psalms.

Fifth motherless child. A girl.
Old enough for embers of memories.
A pride forlorn drives her soul
As, caring for Daddy, she seeks Mam's role.

Their mother-hen father gathers his chicks,
This cock no song to crow.
Insidious germ, fever and pain;
Quick as a shiver, Heaven's gain.

He combs her hair. A final parting.
Vigorous tresses washed from his jug of tears.
The wise, adored eyes he closes,
In hands, life-weathered, a bridal rose.

HENRY GRIFFITHS and family

The Cynon Valley and Nantymoel

There is something protective in the human mind that prevents it from feeling the acuteness of grief until the funeral is over. Henry Griffiths was numbed with shock as he made arrangements for Jane to be buried in Abercynon with their baby daughter. Eight years had passed since they had laid little Catherine Mildred Morgan Griffiths to rest. Harry had lost the great love of his life so quickly and the children were going to be deprived of their mother's love.

All the shopkeepers in Margaret Street closed their doors to show their respect as the little family made their way up to the cemetery. Neighbours drew the curtains in their houses. If Henry Griffiths had any consolation that day, it was the knowledge that the entire community sympathised with him and his children.

The funeral was painfully sad for Henry but, on the same day, he had to face another desperate farewell. In the few days since Jane's death, he had had to gather his thoughts quickly. Nothing would bring Jane back; he was now a working widower and had to consider the children. He would have to carry on managing the shop in Abercynon and supplying the goods for the other businesses. In order to do this, he would need some help with the children but it wouldn't be difficult to employ a local woman to keep an eye on them when he was working. Peggy was nine and almost old enough to look after herself. Nancy was due to start school and Owen would soon begin in the Nursery class. He could send them down to his sister, Sarah, in the school holidays. But he was concerned about the baby. A week earlier, her mother had been feeding her. Now he felt that she needed more than he could provide himself.

Two of the mourners at Jane's funeral were very familiar to Harry. His brother, David, had left Llanwnda for the coal-mines of Nantymoel. David, himself, had been left a widower when his wife, Liza, died of saltpetre poisoning. Harry enjoyed the company of the extended family in Nantymoel and he loved Edwin (Liza's brother), and his wife, Mary. Edwin and Mary had two boys who were almost men and, although Mary was forty years old, she was strong and loving. Edwin and Mary agreed to foster little Nesta and arrangements were quickly made. They would bring her up as if she were their own though Harry would provide for her financially and visit as often as he could. Still in shock, Harry joined the other mourners for some food and drink as he handed the baby over. Mary comforted him.

"*Paid â becso, Harry bach! Edrychwn ni ar ôl y babi.*" (Don't worry, Harry, love. We'll look after the baby.)

From that day onwards, Nesta's home was in Nantymoel. Harry, Mary and Edwin decided that it would be best for her to drop the Griffiths surname and be known as Nesta Harries. This would make life easier when she began school.

Nesta enjoyed her adoptive home with a 'Mam' who was strict but loving. Edwin took the chubby toddler for treats down to the sea-side at Porthcawl but the excitement of such visits was short-lived. Edwin was killed in a colliery explosion and, as a result, the bond between Nesta and her 'Mam' grew even closer. Mary was a very committed chapel-goer and Nesta always went with her. If the weather was too bad to get to the chapel on a Sunday, the two of them held an informal meeting at home. The religious life encouraged more than a love of God – it helped her to develop her innate gifts – singing and poetry. Nesta went on to win many Eisteddfod prizes with her sweet, strong soprano voice. She learnt the rules of Welsh poetry and was soon penning it herself.

All went well until a child came up to Nesta in the school playground. Great truths are often revealed in those little yards – and this child's contribution was no exception.

"Your Mam's dead!" the child taunted.

"No, she's not!" Nesta replied sharply.

All day, these words frightened her and she could hardly wait for the time when school finished and she could check that her Mam was alive and well. She ran home and into Mary's arms. "They told me you were dead!" she wept. "They told me you were dead!"

Mary was now in a difficult and sensitive position. Many of the adults in Nantymoel knew that Nesta was fostered – so a child must have overheard one of them speaking. It was pointless to keep the truth from her now and it was better for Nesta to know what had happened from Mary directly, rather than pick up the whole story from the playground. From then on, Nesta called Harry 'Daddy' and her 'cousins' who came to visit were her brother and sisters. The widowed Mary remained as 'Mam'

Back in Abercynon, Harry tried to deal with his grief. His

success in business seemed cold comfort now. His only joy was the children.

News gets around quickly in small communities and, by the mid nineteen-twenties, everyone in Abercynon was talking about a miracle that had happened over by the Catholic Church. Harry was a devout Welsh Baptist but he wanted to believe this particular story. It seemed that a little boy of three had been rescued from a well that was several feet deep. He insisted that the lady who had helped him out was the very same person as the one he had on the little medal he wore round his neck. This person was the Virgin Mary. The son of Irish people who had come to Wales for the mining, the boy kept to his story even when he was interrogated harshly by priests from all over Britain and Ireland. He was too young to have learnt such details! People began to arrive at the scene in search of healing and they came in great numbers – charabancs were filled with pilgrims and the *Western Mail* hailed Abercynon as the 'Welsh Lourdes'. Miracles were reported in the newspapers.

Harry was worried about Nancy who was still unable to walk properly. He carried her down to the river and lowered his little daughter down into its waters. He persevered and, after a few visits to the 'healing river', Nancy was able to walk normally. Was this a miracle? Was it just the needy child responding to the care and attention of a loving father? Isn't that something of a miracle in itself?

The delight in Nancy's recovery was marred by the mood in the country. It was 1926 and the economy had collapsed. Nobody had any money, unemployment was alarmingly high; Britain had sunk into a Depression. Harry's shops that had been doing so well were now struggling to make any profit. He went round to visit the people who were not paying off their debts. Miners were striking and off work for months without pay. They and their families were hungry and dependent on the soup-kitchens that had been set up in the chapels. Harry was an astute businessman but he had a soft heart and, wherever he went, he heard terrible personal stories. He left their houses, empty-handed. People who had lost husbands and sons in the War were forced to beg. What had happened to the country that made it so unprepared to take care of its people? Harry read the papers, listened to the wireless. The country was certainly in a bad state and there were no signs of a recovery. So much money had been spent on the War that there had to be cut-backs everywhere. Everybody had hoped that America would lend money but it seemed that their economy was bad, too. Harry had left Llanwnda as a young man to find a better life for himself and his wife. Now, everyone around him was finding life more difficult than anything he had known back in his native Pembrokeshire. And Jane, whom he had tried so hard to protect, was dead.

He needed to make quick, sensible decisions. However difficult it was, he came to the conclusion that, for the sake of the children and out of sheer common sense, he would sell the shops. The money would buy him a large house in the bigger town of Aberdare. It needed to be big enough to take in lodgers so that he'd always have an income – and he hoped to find another job. Harry and the children made the move to an elegant, three-storey house in a pleasant part of Aberdare and Harry soon found employment as an Insurance Collector for the Hearts of Oak Benefit Society. He was one of the lucky ones. Nesta was happy and flourishing in Nantymoel and Peggy, Nancy and Owen were doing well at school. They needed a sound education behind them if they were to survive the depression that marred the valley and the whole country.

Then, when they were settled in Aberdare, Henry Griffiths did a strange thing. There were countless men and women who had been left to fend for themselves. So many women had died in pregnancy and child-bearing that there were many widowers around. The First World War had cut into the adult male generation like a cruel knife, leaving a multitude of widows and broken hearts. Henry was a sociable man with a mischievous sense of humour and laughing eyes. The children were a great compensation but they couldn't fill the gap left by Jane's passing. It was a very natural thing for someone in his position to re-marry and that's exactly what he did. It wasn't re-marriage that shocked and surprised everybody. It was his choice of a wife.

Constance Beauchamp was the daughter of a Headmaster from a little village near Hereford. The whole family were members of the High Anglican Church, finding their God in its fragrant incense and ritual. Constance was a very gifted artist who loved to paint oil landscapes on wood. She was also a superb musician and her renditions of classical music on the piano were a joy to hear. She had never married and her father's comfortable middle-class background had enabled her to concentrate on her artistic gifts without needing to worry about earning money. Constance became the second Mrs. Griffiths. In the elegant Victorian home in Aberdare, Harry encouraged Constance to continue practising her music and painting. The language of the home became English and the children didn't find it easy to adapt to all the changes. Harry certainly hadn't chosen Constance to be a mother-figure to them.

Why had he chosen her? Wasn't she the most unlikely wife for this family man with nothing but an elementary education behind him? In many ways, the relationship made sense. Henry Griffiths may have been self-taught but he had many poetry books in his native Welsh and in English. He loved literature, was cultured and well-read. He had learned Esperanto and could discuss all kinds of subjects intelligently. He was sensitive and creative. Admittedly, he had adored Jane and no-one could ever take her place but, in choosing such a different wife the second time, no comparisons would be made to mar the companionship that he sought so much. If Constance's father had offered her a privileged life, Harry would continue to do the same.

History has a habit of shattering the plans that human beings make. In 1939, the Second World War was declared. The coal-mines had enabled Harry to be free of the front line in the First World War and now he was too old to serve in the Second one. However, his son, Owen, was old enough to be called up and so were his daughters' sweethearts. Peggy had left home to study nursing in London and her gentle English fiancé was called up – as was Nancy's fiancé, Lew. Young Nesta was the only one to benefit from the War years – the man who was to be her future husband had come to Nantymoel to work in the pits after he had failed the medical for conscripts. Nancy was training to be a teacher in the college at Swansea so she came home every week-end and, apart from her company, Harry had Constance who, with her piano-playing, transported them for a little while to a land that was free of conflict.

Nancy was a sensitive and slightly vulnerable young woman but Harry was able to calm her anxieties at the week-ends and assure her that all would be well. One week-end, Nancy was in the same room as Constance when the fatal accident happened. Constance bent over to tie the laces of her boots. At first, Nancy thought that her step-mother had just lost her balance and she called out for her father. There was nothing that either of them could do. Without any warning to anybody, Constance had died immediately of a cerebral haemorrhage.

Another funeral had to be organised and a traumatised Nancy had to be persuaded to return to Swansea and continue her studies. There seemed to be no comfort anywhere. The Blitz had begun in London and it seemed as if Hitler was determined to destroy all the major British ports and cities.

The home that had been bought to offer security for the family, was now dismally quiet. There was nothing but the muffled sounds of the lodgers for company. The gregarious and caring Henry Griffiths was alone. The rooms sounded hollow and each empty bedroom was a reminder of the absence of dear ones. The table was too big for a single plate, the piano had fallen silent, there was no-one to share in the simple events of the day and there was a war raging.

Jane was long dead and now Constance had died.

Peggy had settled in London. Harry didn't know then that she would remain in and around London for the rest of her life. That night as he ate alone, Harry just sensed his loneliness.

Owen had been declared missing, presumed dead. Harry didn't know then that Owen would return safely from the War, marry, have three children and live in his wife's native Midlands town. That night as he ate alone, Harry just sensed the loss.

He didn't know then that Nesta would marry the young Cardiganshire farmer she had met in Nantymoel. That night as he ate alone, Harry just felt the gaping hole in his heart.

Nancy was the only home-bird and Harry's big consolation. She had qualified as a teacher in 1940, missing the heavy, fatal bombing in Swansea by months. She looked beautiful for her war-wedding but, as her husband had to return immediately to serve in the Royal Engineers, she remained at home with Harry. He clung onto the hope that she would be able to get a job locally and, indeed, Nancy's first job was in a boys' school in Pontlottyn in the Rhymni Valley. Every morning, she boarded the train that took her to her school and every evening she returned to tell him all about her day. Soon, she had some special news for him. She was expecting a baby. The child was born in his house and she was called Diana. Harry's joy in living returned and he nursed the baby like a mother. Indeed, he often needed to do this because the birth had taken a toll on Nancy's health. When Lew returned from active service in 1945, Harry rejoiced to have the little family living with him but, when they left to live in Essex, he was faced again with loneliness. He tried to make the best of things and had plenty of friends. He went to stay with his children and their families for short periods but he felt that he didn't belong anywhere. When he heard that his sister, Phoebe, needed somewhere to live after retiring from a lifetime in service, Harry decided to return to his roots. The house in Aberdare was sold and he bought a large house in the Main Street in Goodwick. It was another three-storey building with countless rooms, two bathrooms and a long garden to the back that needed strong muscles to climb. This was to remain his home for the rest of his life.

I loved going on holiday to visit Data in Goodwick. My father came sometimes but it was usually me and my mother. We were often there at the same time as an aunt and uncle with their children so I had two cousins for company.

Of course I loved the chance to enjoy myself on the beach like any other child but my favourite times were the evenings. After supper, my mother stayed in the front room with her brother and sister-in-law where they liked to listen to records on the gramophone.

This was my chance to escape into the kitchen where Data was always working. He might be preparing food for the following day, cleaning or cooking – he was always busy because he wanted his family to relax and have everything done for them during their stay. But, whatever he was doing, he had time for me. I had a poor appetite and Data often cooked me a late treat. I loved potato fritters and remember how he made them with the potatoes clean and white and sliced; he dipped each one into the batter that he'd whisked up with a fork and fried them, turning them until they were golden brown on both sides. They were delicious!

When he had a break from work, Data and I sat on the comfy big armchairs and chatted. Those times were wonderful as we talked about important things that were beginning to matter to me – Wales, literature, poetry, life, religion.

I had been learning some Welsh in an earnest effort to regain my roots and knew a few of the hymns. One of them struck a deep chord with me:

Arglwydd Iesu, arwain f'enaid
At y graig sy'n uwch na mi
(Lord Jesus, lead me to the Rock that is higher than me)

"There is a rock that is higher than us, isn't there?" I asked.

"Oh, yes. There is a Rock!" replied Data, with moist eyes," and it's always there!"

I sometimes went with him to chapel on Sunday evenings. The services were entirely in Welsh and I drank them in, even though I couldn't understand it all. Data nudged me softly during the sermon and showed me the little packet of Polos he had in his pocket. He peeled the wrapper down as silently as he could so that a little rounded peppermint with its hole was ready to be taken. I popped it in my mouth and watched as he peeled the foil bit down a little further so that he could have one. Then he folded the wrapper over the next sweet to stop it from getting dirty and the packet went back into his pocket. Whatever Data did, I copied. People often muttered words to show that they agreed with the preacher, offering an 'Amen', a 'Ie, ie' (Hear, hear) or an 'Alleluia'. Because I was sitting so close to Data, I could sense when he was going to speak and I listened carefully as the first sound emerged so that I could rush in and echo his sentiments so closely that it seemed simultaneous.

When my mother and I left Goodwick, Data always booked a taxi to take us to the station even though he lived close enough for us to walk. The last time we visited, everything was the same. The taxi was booked, it arrived, Data came with us, paid the fare and carried our cases into the train and up onto the rack. One thing was different. He usually waited on the station until the train had pulled out and we waved furiously with a handkerchief until we lost sight of each other. On this occasion, he got onto the train to put our cases up but, when he got back onto the platform, he had tears in his eyes and walked away before the train had moved. He didn't look back and I think that, somehow, he must have known that we would never see each other again.

It was Whit Sunday and we hadn't gone down to Wales for the half-term holidays because I had been asked to be a bridesmaid at the wedding of a family friend in Essex on the Monday. We received a telephone call in the morning and my mother began to scream and wail. Data had died unexpectedly but peacefully in his sleep. I didn't know what to do and I certainly didn't feel anything. Instead, I tried to console my mother and told her that Pentecost was a lovely day to die.

Owen and his family were already down in Goodwick and Nesta was still living with her family in Tregaron so the only people who needed to make the long journey down to Wales were Peggy and my mother. My father drove up to fetch Peggy and she stayed overnight with us so that everyone could go to the wedding before the two sisters caught the train for the funeral. I wore a pretty peach dress, had my longish hair swept up into a bouffant style and looked very grown-up. The two bereaved sisters in their black mourning clothes stood out starkly in the church against the elegant wedding outfits and, as I followed the bride out, I gave them a sympathetic smile. I felt nothing at all myself and wondered why I couldn't cry like everyone else.

Nesta was the daughter who had had the least contact with her father, Henry Griffiths, and it is a poignant tribute to his stature and her generosity of spirit that she could write this poem shortly after his death.

'Nhad

Aeth hwn yn grwt dibrofiad o'i enedigol fro
Yng nghefn gwlad Sir Benfro, i'r Sir y 'gweithe glo'
Fe dystia creithiau gleision ei law a'i wyneb e'
I'w waith yng nghrombil daear, ym mhyllau glo y De.

O blith y dynion dwad, a rhai o'i Sir ei hun
Gwnaeth ei ffryndiau cynnar, y rhai'n y dyddiau blin,
A lynodd wrtho'n gadarn, a'r cwlwm aeth yn dynn
Rhwng mab 'Pencaer' Sir Benfro a'r glowyr didwyll hyn.

Yr oedd eu gwaith beunyddiol a'u horiau hamdden hwy
Yn troi ym myd 'y pethau' gan geisio pethau mwy.
Trafodent pennau'r pregeth y bore wedi'r Sul
A byddai dadl bybyr, yn ffas yr haenen gul.

Pa ryfedd i'r gwr ieuanc o'r bwthyn yn y wlad
I dyfu'n wr mor hoffus, ac hefyd cystal tad.
Pan gofiwch mae'n nhymdeithias gwyr dewr y 'geiniog brin'
Y dysgodd gwerthoedd bywyd, y dyddiau cynnar hyn.

Nesta Owen

My Daddy

(A rough translation)

As an inexperienced lad, he left his home
In the heart of Pembrokeshire. Blue scars
On his hand and his face bore witness to that work
In the depths of the earth, in the pits of the South.

He made close friendships with the men
Who came from far and wide,
The bonds were deep and strong between
Those workers and the lad from 'Pencaer'.

As they worked so hard, so long, they tried
To make the world a better place, to seek for higher things.
With lively discussion there in the narrow seams,
They analysed Sunday's sermon.

How amazing that the young man from a country cottage
Should become such a loveable man and a wonderful father,
Remember it was there, early on, in the company
Of those brave men, that he learnt the true value of life.

PHOEBE ANN HENNER (NANCY) GRIFFITHS and LEWIS WILLIAM WILLIAMS at Aberdare

As October approached in 1942, the war-time heaviness was lightened in Aberdare. Preparations were being made for a wedding.

Nancy Griffiths never liked her full name of Phoebe Ann Henner but she had to use it during the marriage service in Bethel Baptist Chapel, Abernant. With the help of her brother's fiancée, a wedding-dress was sent down on loan for her to wear. Leave was arranged for her fiancé, Lewis (Lew) William Williams, who was serving abroad in the Royal Engineers. Outfits for all the extended family were bought, made or borrowed. Henry Griffiths had recently lost his second wife, Constance, so his eldest daughter, Peggy, stood in as the bride's mother.

The day came and the couple's joy was tangible. Harry looked smart as he prepared to give his daughter away. Although Lew's career as a teacher was on hold during the War, there were great prospects ahead for him in the future.

And the groom? Who *was* this handsome, dark-haired young man with the sultry good looks of a Mediterranean? He was the only son of Tom and Jinnie Williams of Aberdare.

Nancy Griffiths (my mother). A photograph to cheer her fiancé, Lew, in wartime. 1940.

Lew Williams (my father). A wartime photo for his fiancée, Nancy.

Nancy and Lew Williams on their wedding-day. October 10th, 1942.
Aberdare. Back row: Tom Williams (groom's father/Daddy Bom),
Rees Williams (Tom's brother), Lewis Williams (groom/my father),
Nancy Williams (bride/my mother), Henry Griffiths (bride's father/
Data), Danny Wells (husband to groom's cousin). Front row: Jinnie
Williams (groom's mother/Nana), Iris (bridesmaid/bride's college
friend), Margaret Wells (Gwendo and Danny's daughter), Nesta
(bridesmaid/bride's sister), Peggy (bride's sister, 'standing-in' for bride's
mother).

The WILLIAMS family

John WILLIAMS m. ?
b.1800 Abercanaid
Haulier

William LLEWELYN m. **Margaret**
b.1800 Margam   b.1800
Coal-miner

Tabitha   David
b.1821   1826

Lewis WILLIAMS — m. — **Kezziah LLEWELYN**
b.1824 Abercanaid   b.1827 Abercanaid
Haulier

Lewis LEWIS m. **Elizabeth MEREDITH**
b.1839 Llandeilo | b.1844 Llangadog
Coal-miner/Heater in Ironworks

Martha William Margaret Lewis Kezziah MaryAnn Elizabeth
b.1848 1850   1856   1859   1860   1863   1872

Thomas Margaret   Elizabeth Lewis William Suzannah
b.1867   1869   1872   1875   1881

John WILLIAMS   m.   **Ann LEWIS**
b.1866 Abercanaid Coal-miner   b.1870 Abercanaid

LizabethAnn   Lewis John   Kezziah   Rees   Blodwen   Margaret May (Maggie)
b.1886   b.1890   1892   1894   b1896   b.1899

Thomas WILLIAMS
b. 1892 Abercanaid Coal-miner   m. **Jennet Lewis**. b.1890 Aberdare

Lewis William WILLIAMS b.1917 Aberdare. Teacher m. Phoebe Ann Henner (Nancy) GRIFFITHS b.1919

Diana Gruffydd WILLIAMS m. Peter Huw MORGAN
b.1944   b.1945

John and Ann (née Lewis) Williams and family. Back row: Rees, Lizabeth Ann, Lewis John, Tom (Daddy Bom), Kezziah. Seated – John and Ann Williams. Front row: Blodwen, a nephew, Margaret May (Maggie) c. 1904.

Tom Williams (Daddy Bom) as a young man(seated) with friend.

Daddy Bom and me. Graig mountain, Aberdare c. 1952

DADDY BOM

When, as a young child, I first heard the name Tom, *I tried to say it myself. It came out as 'Bom'. The name stuck.* Tom Williams *was always my 'Daddy Bom'.*

He and my grandmother lived in a little miner's terraced house in the heart of Aberdare and I enjoyed my holidays with them there. It was Daddy Bom who came upstairs when I couldn't settle at night. He always smiled at me as though I made him really happy. He moved his fingers against the light to make shadows in the shape of animals – there was the swan, the rabbit, the butterfly, the dog... We both laughed at these – especially when he added the noises or had a little story to tell about them. I tried to copy the shapes with my own hands but I was never as good as he was. Sometimes, if he had a bit of string, he'd tie the two ends together and hold the piece on his wrists before winding it around his fingers to make a cat's cradle. I then had to try to get it onto my own hand by using a sort of web-like pattern, then he had to get it back onto his own hand – and so it went on until the string ended up in a muddle and we had to start again.

I was a poor eater and most of the efforts made to coax me during the day, failed. But, in the evenings, Daddy Bom made me toast which was delicious! Smiling at me, he'd take a slice of bread and puncture it with a fork before placing it in front of the coal fire. He drew it away from time to time to see how well it had browned and it was always striped by the grilles of the fire. When the toast was ready, I spread it with a lump of Welsh salty butter and, as I did so, some of it dribbled down the little holes made by the fork. It tasted wonderful!

When I was quite young, Daddy Bom was still able to work. I remember him coming home with his clothes, face and hands so black that I was frightened. It wasn't the dirt that scared me – it was the sight of Daddy Bom's eyes with rims that were so red and sore that they looked unreal against the black coal dust. He soon had the tin bath filled with hot water for him and, as he scrubbed himself with green soap, he became my Daddy Bom again! When he stepped out of the bath, he put a towel around his waist and smiled. His eyes were still red but they didn't scare me when he had clean skin.

It wasn't long before he was too ill to work in the pits at all. He had a nystagmus (an eye condition that many miners contracted after years of working in the darkness) but, worse than this, he had the dreaded 'dust' – the word that everybody whispered. For a coal-miner, having the 'dust' – pneumoconiosis – was the worst thing that could happen. Daddy Bom worked for a while mowing the tennis courts in Aberdare. I loved to go with him, playing on the grass as he went up and down in a little machine, waving at me whenever he passed. On our way back home, we'd usually sit on a bench for him to have one of his Woodbines. The cigarettes came in little green packets of five and Daddy Bom smoked them right down to the end. When there was hardly anything left, he cupped his hand with its yellowed fingers around the stub as if he were cradling it. I wondered if he would burn himself but he never did.

The awful thing about the 'dust' was the coughing. When Daddy Bom was too ill to work at all, Nana (my grandmother) had to work as a school-cleaner. I remember how Daddy Bom tried to help her one day by carrying a bucket of coal down for her from the coal-shed. As we walked down the school-yard, he had to put his load down and the coughing began. It was something that seemed to affect his whole body and, as the bout built up, his face changed colour from grey to red and purple with the veins sticking out as if they were angry. He reached for his handkerchief and spat the phlegm onto it before wiping his wet forehead with the back of his hand. He looked at me and I wanted to cry because he had that lovely smile even though he was exhausted and ashamed that he had been unable to carry the filled bucket. He looked so tired and helpless! Why couldn't doctors make him better?

Every afternoon, he had to go to bed for a rest; he called this 'going to have a spell'. Again, he always smiled at me as he went, pulling the curtain back that kept the draught from coming downstairs before he unlocked the little catch that kept the door in place – and he was gone.

The catch was put back in place and the curtain was closed again so he was locked upstairs for an hour or so. I was always pleased when I heard him coming down the stairs, knocking on the door to be let out. It seemed such a lonely thing to have to do.

Daddy Bom enjoyed talking to people and he often sat on a little stool on the front door step so that he could chat to passers-by. I liked to stand around and listen. There was usually a lot of laughter but, whenever they got talking about something called politics, people got angry and raised their voices. I knew that the conversation was coming to an end when Daddy Bom came out with the words that meant he had had enough of politics. "There's only been one honest man to go to Parliament," he said, "And that was Guy Fawkes!"

Daddy Bom and I spent a lot of time together, walking. We went along the dram road – the dusty dram road with black earth that was full of wild flowers at its side. I got to know the ferns and the heather and picked the beautiful, white phlox with its lovely smell to take home as a bouquet for Nana.

We often went for a couple of miles down the dram road to see my uncle and his family. On our way, we passed a stream that tumbled down in a little waterfall at a place called Maes-y-Ffynnon. Daddy Bom showed me how to cup my hands together and place them on the edge of the running water so that I could catch some of it to drink. The trick was getting my hand up to my mouth before it all spilt out. The water was always icy-cold, even in the summer, and left my hands red and tingling – but it was all worth it because those sips of water somehow tasted better than anything that came from a tap.

We had to make our own way back home after the visits too so I tended to get tired. If Daddy Bom saw me dawdling behind him on our return journey, he turned around to face me with a smile – that lovely, sad smile! He held his hand out to beckon me on. There were no buses or cars, of course, so there was nothing we could do but carry on walking. To encourage me, he always sang the same song.

"If I give you the keys to Heaven, if I give you the keys to Heaven,

"Madam, will you walk, Madam, will you talk,

"Madam, will you walk and talk with me?"

He held out his hand and, somehow, with his hand in mine, I always found the energy to catch up with him and sing the reply,

"If you give me the keys to Heaven, If you give me the keys to Heaven,

"Yes, I will walk, Yes, I will talk,

"Yes, I will walk and talk with thee"

And off we went to finish our journey.

The WILLIAMS family in Abercanaid

The Williams family had been enjoying the New Year celebrations as usual. The children had been up early, decorating apples with raisins and sprigs of holly (*calennig*) to take round to the houses in the village. As they knocked on the doors, they'd sung greetings and received a penny or a piece of cake for their efforts. They had all heard the knocking on their own door when the Mari Lwyd came and they enjoyed the amusing verses they all sang before letting everybody in. They had seen it all before, of course – the horse's skull with its snapping jaw, the man hidden by a sheet who held the Mari Lwyd in place with a pole, the ribbons, the fiddlers, the fun and the food they all shared together afterwards. All these customs were familiar but there was something special about this New Year that none of them had *ever* seen before. On this January morning, cold and cheerless though it was, a new century was beginning. They all wondered what 1800 and the nineteenth century would bring. Would the world change for the better? Feelings of excitement and hope were mingled with a natural fear and worry. They had already seen so many changes.

After the festivities and the food, the older folk were in a good mood as they reminisced amongst themselves. They remembered how things had been when Abercanaid was nothing more than a little hamlet close to a couple of other villages called Merthyr Tydfil and Troedyrhiw. They smiled as they recalled the good harvests and the simple life of tending to the cattle and sheep. Life had always been hard – they had not forgotten how it took years to recover from a season of bad crops, disease in the animals or a dry summer. Of course, they had known about the ironstone in the land then because people had been using it for ages. So many trees had been felled to make the charcoal for the furnaces that they had been forbidden to cut any more down. But now, it seemed that they were getting round the problem by roasting coal into coke. It was all too complicated and they returned to their memories.

The younger adults had different concerns. They were the ones who had to live and work in this area that was changing so quickly that they could hardly take it all in! Merthyr Tydfil was only two miles away and now it had become the largest town in the whole of Wales! Ten thousand people! Their isolated village was merging into the bigger town now as influential men with money had come in to set up the huge, noisy Ironworks. A big problem with the iron had been the fact that it was heavy to transport but now a canal had been built to take it down to the little port of Cardiff. There was talk of a new dram-road being built to take it down from Penydarren to Abercynon as well. Everything was getting bigger and busier and there were even more blast-furnaces coming to Merthyr. All the time, there seemed to be some news of a change here – or a change there – and, with wars being waged against the French, iron was in greater demand than ever. More and more men were arriving from the country to take up the jobs.

For a moment, the Williams family fell silent in the early hours of that January morning and turned to look at their youngest member. There was a new baby boy in his crib; his name was John.

"What will life hold for you in this new century, little one?" his mother whispered. "Will Merthyr and Abercanaid just carry on growing? Will you have a good future with all these riches in our soil?

They didn't have long to wait for the answer.

JOHN WILLIAMS at Abercanaid

Little John Williams was working by the age of eight. By this time, Merthyr was producing forty-five thousand tons of iron a year and, apart from men, women and children were needed to help out in the industry. There was no chance of schooling for young John, of course, and he was more than capable of doing lighter tasks in the Ironworks. There was no time to complain and his small wage was welcomed.

Life revolved around his work and the years passed quickly. John became a man. With the industrial boom dominating the area, he remained in Abercanaid. When it was his turn to marry, John and his wife lived and worked by following what was becoming the traditional pattern in the Valleys. The man's job was to work for the heavy industries whilst his wife produced children, looked after the home and taught the next generation how to repeat everything in a similar way. What else was there to do in the area?

Abercanaid had kept its village spirit of community even though it had become an extension of Merthyr in many ways. With the huge demand for accommodation, continuous rows of terraced houses merged the two places into one. But everyone knew their neighbours and John was walking home from work one evening with William Llewelyn. There had only been one subject on everyone's lips for months.

Conditions had been so bad for working men that things had come to a head now in 1831. Riots had just broken out in Merthyr, with hundreds of their friends and colleagues marching down to the Court of Requests building in the town. This was where records of debts were kept and checked before the bailiffs were sent out to repossess the belongings of the ordinary people like them who had no chance of repaying. The men were determined to fight for justice and the rioting had been so spirited that troops were sent down to tackle the angry workers. There had been a scuffle outside the Castle Inn, the troops panicked and began to fire randomly. When news got round that innocent people had died and were injured, most of the working men for miles around in Glamorganshire and Monmouthshire had left their work to show their support. They were well-organised and passionate and emotions had been running so high in nearby Hirwaun that a calf was killed and a banner dipped in its blood. The men lifted it up and called it the 'Red Flag'. Fearing that they were losing control, the police acted swiftly by raiding local houses and they brought twenty people to trial. Ten men and two women were transported and one man was hanged. His name was Richard Lewis but John and William knew him as Dic Penderyn.

And it was Dic Penderyn who was occupying the minds of John Williams and William Llewelyn that evening.

"Have you heard the news about Dic?" John Williams asked, with a grim expression on his face.

William's face was sad. "Aye, they hanged him in Cardiff jail. Poor man!"

"They just wanted someone to blame!" said John angrily.

"A nice man he was, too. He hadn't done anything wrong! They tried to say that he stabbed a soldier outside the Castle Inn…"

John broke in passionately, "But he swore he didn't do it! We *knew* Dic!" Quieter now, he added, "Did you hear what Dic's last words were before they hanged him in Cardiff jail?"

"No?" William turned round quickly to face John. This was something new!

"'Arglwydd, dyma gamwedd' (Lord, this is wrong), that's what he said! Poor Dic!"

William was shocked. "Dear, dear," he muttered. "May he rest in peace! An innocent man hanged and twelve people transported to the other side of the world!" He thought about it all for a moment then said with determination, "But they don't know what we're made of! We'll *never* forget Dic Penderyn"

The two men parted company as they reached their homes. They were good pals and they didn't know then that their lives would become even more closely linked.

John's son, Lewis, went on to work for some time as a haulier with his father. It had been his task to drive the horses and tram away from the wall-face where the colliers were picking the coal and to look after the horses. The animals had to be fed and, then, when his long shift was over, he had to lead them home. Young boys and girls were always very popular in the mines because their small and flexible bodies fitted into the small, narrow places that the grown men couldn't manage. In the winter, Lewis left for work before dawn, spent the day in the eerie darkness of the mine then, when he had led the horses home, it was already night. The conditions underground were dangerous for father and son and, like the others, they came home with bruises and cuts but were grateful that there was nothing worse – men died in explosions, lads lost their limbs. There wasn't a great deal of spare time for Lewis but courting always seems to find a way. He fell in love with a young neighbour. Kezziah was the daughter of William and Margaret Llewelyn.

WILLIAM AND MARGARET LLEWELYN

From Margam to Abercanaid

Margaret Llewelyn was shocked when her husband, William, told her the news about Dic Penderyn. What a terrible ending to the fight to bring some fairness to the lives of the working people of Merthyr.

"They were so crafty!" William said, angrily. "They changed their minds about the other man, Lewis Lewis! First of all, they said that they'd sentence him to death too! But he was the ring-leader so they thought that they'd please everybody by letting him go! If Lewis had been hanged, they worried that we'd all carry on with the riots. Well, they made a mistake if they thought that they'd teach us a lesson by taking it out on poor Dic!"

Margaret had heard it all before but she knew how angry everyone was and it was better to give vent to it than take to drink. She was angry, herself, to see how lives of whole families had been ruined. She thought about the way things had worked out and, saddened though she was by the dreadful news, things couldn't have stayed as they had been. They had come to Abercanaid from Margam in search of work and William had been so pleased to get a job working with the iron at first. But how could they carry on without people making a stand about the awful conditions? Dic Penderyn had suffered them, of course, and he had paid the price with his life.

William moved on to become a coal-miner. He worked for twelve hours a day underground and then there was the journey to and from home on top of that. The labour was hard and some of his friends had lost their lives. Others were so badly injured that they couldn't support themselves or their families. There were frequent accidents, the only light came from candles and it was all a terrible strain on the eyes. There was the wetness and the constant risk from falling coal; there were explosions. He was angry that he was paid partly in vouchers for the Tommie shops – it was so unjust! These Tommie shops – the truck system – caught them all in a trap! They all had to use these vouchers in exchange for goods in shops that belonged to the owners of the collieries and ironworks. *They* were getting richer all the time in their big houses! Their own houses had been built so quickly that no-one had had the time to think about sanitation and they were all overcrowded with several people sharing a bed. If there was an outbreak of disease, it was hard to stop it spreading throughout the family. No, Merthyr was not a good place to live anymore! Many of his friends spent their wages in the public houses. No-one could blame them, really! They just drank their money away to try and forget about the misery of it all! But it was ruining lives! What with the anger and the alcohol, there were brawls in the streets and the poor wives were desperate. Some of them were beaten and the children weren't getting fed.

Yes, action had been necessary. And they would never forget Dic Penderyn! William and Margaret looked at their three young children – Tabitha, David and Kezziah. A devout couple, they prayed that life would be easier for them because of the Riots – and they remembered Dic's family and the people who had been transported.

LEWIS WILLIAMS and KEZZIAH LLEWELYN at Abercanaid

Kezziah Llewelyn was just seventeen when she made her way up to the Parish Church in Merthyr Tydfil for her wedding. It was 1843 and her groom, Lewis Williams, had turned twenty. In the Bible, Kezziah, one of Job's daughters, was renowned for her beauty and, as far as Lewis was concerned, his bride had been well-named! He had already been working for fourteen years as a haulier but his wages had gone to his father. Now, as a married man and a collier, his earnings would finally be his own so that he could support himself and Kezziah in their little terraced house in Abercanaid.

There was plenty of work in and around Merthyr Tydfil, which was at the height of its success – so employment was not a problem. Their parents had told them all about the misery that led to the riots and the martyrdom of Dic Penderyn – but life was still hard.

Lewis worked long hours in a dirty job and saw no daylight in the winter and just a little sun in the summer months – just like his father. He came home black from the coal-dust so a good supply of water was needed every day. Kezziah collected all the rainwater, of course, and she was able to use the Canaid brook but it wasn't enough, especially after a dry spell. Kezziah had to rely on the water from the well and she made the journey to fetch it almost every day. They had a lodger to cater for as well so, when the first baby arrived, water was needed for four people. Kezziah set off for the well with the baby wrapped round her in a blanket. Sometimes, especially in the summer, the queue was so long that she couldn't even see its beginning but Kezziah had no choice but to stand and wait. The women shuffled forward slowly and the baby became restless. Kezziah gave her breast, hoping and praying that her milk supply wouldn't dry up. The little one, snug inside the blanket, settled.

A couple of hours passed by and the sun rose higher into the sky. Waiting at the well was more pleasant in the summer but the heat meant that there was a risk of it running dry. In the winter, she felt the bitter winds and the rain chilling her body – but they couldn't live without water. There was some more movement and Kezziah was relieved to see that it was almost her turn to fill her jug. At last, she made her way home, taking care not to spill anything. Even after the long delays, the water from the well didn't look too clean and it smelt bad after a day in the house. Nevertheless, every drop was precious!

As more babies arrived, the older children took their turn at fetching the water but the job sometimes fell to the lodger who was none other than Kezziah's own mother, Margaret Llewelyn. Kezziah's father, William, had died, leaving her mother destitute. The life-span of a coal-miner was often cut short and families had to manage as well as they could. Without her husband's wages, Margaret was penniless and she had no assets at all. What would become of her? At first, she was able to stay at home because her son, David, was working as a coal-miner and bringing some wages home. But, when the time came for David to marry, Margaret was unable to keep her home and was declared a pauper. She was spared from the Workhouse when she went to lodge with her youngest, married daughter.

Living with a grandmother in the house was an advantage in many ways for Kezziah. Apart from queuing up at the well, Margaret was very familiar with all the old lullabies and she knew how to relieve that miserable problem of infant colic! The children were all given traditional family names so there was a Lewis and a Kezziah (after their parents) and a Margaret, William and John (after their grandparents) as well as a Martha, MaryAnn and Elizabeth. The family moved with their eight children to a slightly bigger house in Nightingale Street.

Merthyr was still a bustling industrial centre but the peak of the iron industry was over as Lewis approached middle-age. He was a capable man and had never been without work but he changed his job according to the town's mixed fortunes – there was a slump one year and an up-turn the next. After his early days as a haulier, he had moved on to be a collier and had seen improvements – he felt safer with a Davey lamp and it certainly gave Kezziah greater peace of mind too. But, then, after twenty years underground, Lewis looked after horses again – but as an ostler this time and not a haulier. Strangely enough, just as the great iron industry in Merthyr began to decline in the 1870s, Lewis went to work there for the first time. The dangers of the daily work in the dark seams were replaced by the almost unbearable levels of heat in the furnaces. Lewis was a tough man.

Kezziah was devoted to her family and determined to do the best for them. Shuddering at the memory of what had happened to her mother, she joined a Friendly Society. By paying in a small sum regularly, she'd be entitled to some money if she or Lewis became ill and, if she or Lewis died, the Society would ensure that they had a decent funeral. Would life ever get any easier? All the children were working now and it seemed such a poor reward to have to return to a home that couldn't provide the most basic of human needs. It took outbreaks of typhoid and cholera in Merthyr before anything was done to improve matters. At last, every household was promised a proper water supply so the days of the queues at the well would be a thing of the past. Lime was provided so that everybody could disinfect their walls – and sewers were planned! Maybe there was going to be some justice and fairness for good working-class people at last.

Kezziah needed to hold on to this belief for the sake of her children. They were all working by this time, of course. The boys expected to have tough, physically demanding jobs – but the girls in the family were not exempt from them either. Even with the coming of the railways, the canal was still used so Martha went to work there as a dock labourer and Margaret was a labourer at the coal-works. William was a haulier and Lewis and Kezziah's youngest son, John, was sent down the coal-mines as a boy too. Kezziah was kept busy preparing food for them all to take to work and she made sure that Lewis and the boys had their supplies in little tins. The day's work was hard and she didn't want the mice and rats underground reaching the precious bread and cheese before them.

John, born in 1866, was a strong, robust and handsome lad with a mass of black hair and swarthy good looks. Volatile and strong-minded, he had a hearty appetite for life and, when he became a man, he was lucky enough to find the ideal wife. Ann Lewis loved him but she also had qualities to balance and complement John's hearty vitality. She was the daughter of another couple who had left the poverty in rural West Wales in search of work. Her parents, Lewis and Elizabeth Lewis, had settled in Abercanaid but Elizabeth was nowhere to be seen on the day that her lovely, gentle daughter, Ann, was wed.

LEWIS LEWIS of Llandeilo
and ELIZABETH MEREDITH of Llangadog

The beautiful county of Carmarthenshire has rolling hills and rich, fertile soil but, with the coming of the nineteenth century, there were fewer and fewer people who were able to benefit from it. Large landowners were buying up the land from the smaller farmers who were struggling to make ends meet. For the agricultural labourer who owned no land at all, life was becoming impossible.

When Lewis Lewis was born in Llandeilo in 1839, his loving parents knew that he would probably have to move away. They did their best to take care of him as a child and the pain of parting was softened by the knowledge that the new industries in the South would provide him with a roof over his head and food to fill his belly.

Lewis left the pretty little town of Llandeilo for the coal-mines of Merthyr Tydfil but he didn't make the journey alone. His younger brother, William, had decided to join him and they were astounded as their eyes saw the very different landscape of the town that was to be their new home. At first, they lodged in a little terraced house where they shared a rented room with some other young colliers. At least they had the chance to talk together after the bath they took in front of the coal fire at the end of the day.

With the worst of the grime cleaned off, the two brothers chatted about all that had happened to them during the day. How much money should they send home to Llandeilo? Had there been any falling coal today? Had there been any injuries? Should they go to one of the taverns in the town? How they missed their family and the fresh air of the countryside! They examined each other's bruises and cuts and tended to them, remembering the old remedies from home and, as miners, they were getting used to treating their own wounds anyway. They bathed their troubled eyes that had struggled to work in the darkness and were so glad to be together, helping each other through the early days. However, it didn't take them long to build up close friendships with the other miners – it was impossible to work together in danger for twelve hours a day and not share an intimate bond! The two brothers were soon ready to move on independently.

Lewis returned to Carmarthenshire to marry his sweetheart. Elizabeth Meredith, from Llangadog, had been helping out at home and on the land until Lewis came back for her with accommodation arranged in Abercanaid. He had already warned her of the challenges and the different way of life in the Valleys but he had spared her some of the details of its danger. She would find out soon enough!

The newly-wed couple moved into a little, rented terraced house by the canal. Elizabeth certainly worried about Lewis every day as he set off for his dangerous work but she was concerned about another matter – and that was the language.

The couple had never spoken anything but Welsh and, when their children arrived, they naturally expected to carry on with the tradition. Elizabeth had only just left Carmarthenshire and, although she hadn't been to school, she had learnt a lot in the chapel and knew long passages from the Bible by heart – in *Welsh*. She knew all the simple, old lullabies and how could anyone use a word other than *cwtch* with a little one who needed a cuddle?

Lewis and Elizabeth knew that there had been bitterness over the years about the language but it hadn't mattered to them until now. In the sixteenth century, it seemed that there had been an Act of Union from the government that said that a Welshman could only have equal rights with an Englishman if he gave up his language. Many of the rich landowners and the gentry had been only too happy to do this – but Lewis and Elizabeth and their families had never *expected* to have equal rights with Englishmen so they just carried on speaking their own, loved language. There had never been a problem – until now.

Here in Merthyr, Lewis was working with men who had come from all over the place to work – from Somerset, Gloucestershire and Devon. They were good men and Elizabeth had nothing against them at all but they *did* speak English. The miners needed to work together especially if there was any danger underground and the language they tended to use was English. Elizabeth's neighbours spoke English just like their husbands. Of course, there were plenty of Welsh miners who had come from rural areas in search of work like themselves. It was tempting just to mix with them but this mining community was close and there was no room for division. Elizabeth and Lewis didn't want to condemn neighbours just because they were English and spoke their own language – but how could they safeguard their own tongue that had already been so battered and threatened?

When her first babies arrived, Elizabeth spoke to them all in Welsh. Thomas, Margaret, Ann and Elizabeth were all born within the space of five years and heard nothing but the lilting Celtic tongue but, when Elizabeth returned home to Llangadog to have her fifth child, Lewis William, in 1875, things had changed.

Elizabeth talked to her relatives about her new life in the South.

"No, the oldest children don't go to school in Merthyr," she explained "but they are learning passages from the Bible in Sunday School in Welsh!"

"Good!"

"Yes," Elizabeth assured her family "the little ones go regularly to chapel!" But her voice changed tone as she added, "Of course, we all know about the new problem!"

A new law had been passed five years earlier which meant that all children had to have elementary education. It had taken a few years to put it into practice but the new baby – and any future babies – would have to go to school. Their lessons would be in English.

The women of the family worried and whispered together. "Have you heard about the cruelty in the playgrounds of these new schools?"

"Yes!" Elizabeth knew well what they were talking about. "When the little ones are out playing in the yard, they really do have to speak English there – and, if a child is caught speaking Welsh, he has to wear a board around his neck. When somebody else is heard speaking Welsh, the board is passed on to the next child and the poor mite who's wearing the board when the bell rings, is punished."

How had all this happened? Why couldn't they leave the little ones alone? What harm were they doing by speaking Welsh? The family reckoned that it had all started after some English inspectors had come down to Wales and sent bad reports back to the government. They had said that everyone was backward – and they blamed it all on the language. Their accounts hadn't been called the Treason of the Blue Books for nothing! But what could they all do about it? As Elizabeth prepared to make her way back to Abercanaid, she promised her family that she and Lewis would carry on doing what they had always done.

"The language at home will always be Welsh!" she said, as she kissed them good-bye.

Back in the grime of industrial Merthyr, Lewis had changed his job. Although the iron industry was now declining, Lewis went on to work there as a heater. Labour in the fresh air of the Carmarthenshire countryside of his youth had failed to earn him a living so he had exchanged it for the narrow, black seams below the earth where he never saw daylight at all in the winter. Now he was exchanging the darkness for the almost unbearable, choking white heat at the Ironworks. It affected his eyes badly and after years of trying to work in the dark, he now had to work in such a bright light that he was unable to see properly by the end of the day.

Time passed and the biggest consolation for the couple was their children. Lewis and Elizabeth were *so* proud of them. Thomas had already left home, Margaret and Elizabeth were working as general domestics, Lewis William was a coal-miner and little Susannah was just seven and still at school. Their daughter, Ann, was engaged to be married. The wedding between Ann Lewis and the handsome John Williams took place on a summer's day in July, 1887. Happy as the bride was, there were tears in Ann's eyes when she was caught unguarded that day. Her father, Lewis, looked strained and his wife, Elizabeth, was not present at all.

Elizabeth was at home in their little terraced house by the canal, seriously ill with consumption – tuberculosis. The family had tried to care for her over the past months and, in so doing, were all at risk of catching the disease themselves. For Elizabeth, there was no escape to the country or the mountains; there was nowhere for her to suffer but at home. Some people said that this dreaded disease came about through dirtiness and poverty so there was a shame and stigma to add to the pain. No-one could have been cleaner than this family who did the very best they could in the circumstances. Ann had nursed her mother lovingly and tenderly. They had turned to all the old herbs – the Horehound and Coltsfoot that were good for coughs. Although they *did* help to bring up some of the phlegm, the illness progressed and the family just focused their attention on making Elizabeth comfortable. A cordial made from borage flowers had lifted her spirits but, for all their efforts, Elizabeth just got thinner and paler and weaker.

Elizabeth was delighted that Ann was going to marry the strong, virile John Williams and, as their new home was going to be in the cottage next door, the family wouldn't lose this sweet girl.

Sometimes, people who are dying hang on for a particular reason before they are able to let go. Elizabeth lived to know that her daughter had married and Lewis signed the certificate as a proud witness. On the following day, he was at Elizabeth's side as she died.

Gweddi Elizabeth Lewis

Amddiffyna fy ngwr rhag pob salwch,
Amddiffyna fy mhlant rhag pob salwch,
Amddiffyna fi.

Amddiffyna fy ngwr rhag fy haint,
Amddiffyna fy mhlant rhag fy haint,
Amddiffyna fi.

Amddiffyna fy ngwr hebddof i
Amddiffyna fy mhlant hebddof i,
Derbyn fi i'r Deyrnas Di.

Elizabeth Lewis' Prayer

Protect my husband from all disease,
Protect my children from all disease,
Protect me.

Protect my husband from my disease,
Protect my children from my disease,
Protect me.

Protect my husband without me,
Protect my children without me,
Receive me into Thy Kingdom.

After the funeral, Lewis Lewis carried on with his life as a coal-miner. Elizabeth's illness had taken a lot out of them all. No-one would take her place but now he had to concentrate on sharing his home with his younger children. Lewis William, at fifteen, had been working down in the pit for some time so there was some extra money coming home. Father and son had a lot in common now and Ann and her new husband were only separated by a wall!

JOHN and ANN WILLIAMS
at Abercanaid and Cwmaman

At nineteen, the newly-married John Williams was an experienced collier who had already been working for over ten years in the pits. He was a strong man in every way and his powerful muscles served him well. For her part, seventeen-year old Ann proved to be an excellent wife who did everything she could to ensure that the cupboard was full at home. This wasn't always easy and, as John had such a hearty appetite, he often drank a pint or so of water before his morning shift to fully stretch his stomach – it was hard to go down in the shaft with pangs of hunger. Children came and Ann was as tender a mother as she was a wife. Elizabeth Ann was born first in 1889, then Lewis John arrived the following year and they were blessed with another son, Thomas, in 1892.

As another century was drawing to a close, life was still incredibly difficult for the miners and their families. In spite of the Davey lamps, accidents and explosions still happened and it was hard to watch the men turn pale from lack of daylight. Ann watched every morning from the front-door step and waved as John set out for work in his heavy clothes and strong, nailed boots. He met up with his friends on the way to work before they queued up to get their lamp and huddled together to pile into the cage. It took a few minutes to get used to the darkness in the pit. The woollen clothing and moleskin trousers had been welcome outside but they became cumbersome after an hour or two of hacking at the coal. However, their thickness, along with the leathers strapped over the knees, were the best protection he had against falling coal and the constant threat of injury. John had learnt how to identify every sound – the trundling of the tracks, the other men hammering, the water trickling down, timbers cracking, the scuttling of the mice that kept them company. The horses had a good sense of danger and, if they were nervous, John knew they were in trouble. The water drunk in the morning to top his breakfast didn't fool his stomach for long and he was always ready to eat his tin of provisions in the middle of the day and drink the can of tea. But, once he had swallowed them down, John didn't waste any more time. He was paid by the amount of coal he could free up to the wagons so every minute was precious.

Even in the Valleys during those productive years, work could not be taken for granted. For a while, in the early eighteen-nineties, John worked as an ostler with the horses, then he was offered a new job back down in the coal-mines – but not in Abercanaid! The family would have to move to Cwmaman – a village on the outskirts of Aberdare. This was no distance at all really, the people of Cwmaman gave them a warm welcome and they soon settled into their new terraced house in a street called Prospect Place. It was well-named. As they looked out from the front-door step, they could see the Colliery itself in one direction but when their eyes turned the other way, they faced the high, black, brooding mountain that somehow lifted the spirits.

Ann had four more babies in Cwmaman – Kezziah, Rees, Blodwen and Margaret May (Maggie): the Williams' family were now a lively and interesting brood. As the children's personalities developed, John continued his dangerous work in the mines but Ann's life was no easy matter either. Apart from bringing up the children, she had to wash the clothes, clean and bake. Monday was usually washing-day but Ann soon had four lots of working-clothes to attend to – Lewis John, Thomas (Tom) and Rees all followed in their father's footsteps and became coal-miners when they were little more than boys. The clothes were often stiff from the sweat, the dust and water that had seeped into them underground so she boiled them up with soda before taking them, one by one, to scrub against her board with the soap that made her hands so red and sore. Then she turned them through the mangle that squeezed most of the water out so that the clothes wouldn't need too much drying. Drying was only a big problem if the weather was bad and there was certainly plenty of rain! On wet days, she had to line everything up above the coal fire or *anywhere* in the warm kitchen. Working-clothes had to be clean and dry for the next shift. Ann didn't complain. She had a husband who was still in work and healthy despite the years he had spent in the dark, narrow seams. She had a roof over her head, her working boys were healthy and contributing to the family's income. Her four lively daughters were strong.

The only thing that really alarmed Ann was the hooter that sounded at the Colliery when there was an accident underground. When she heard it, she dropped whatever she was doing and ran to the colliery to watch and wait. It was the waiting that was worse than anything else as she and the other women stood – often too anxious to talk. They craned their necks as soon as there was any sound or movement to see if the man on the stretcher was one of theirs. When a woman recognised a loved one, she usually cried or screamed and ran up to him – but sometimes she stood still, pale, and paralysed by the shock. Ann always did what she could to comfort and help before going home and thanking God that John and her boys had been spared. No-one knew what tomorrow would bring but there was no point in worrying about it. Anyway, she took all her concerns to her God in Seion Chapel.

John and Ann remained in their little terraced house in Cwmaman for the rest of their lives.

Cân Ann Williams

Mae'n nhw'n dod adre' yn frwnt,
Fy nynion i.
Y dyn a roddodd fodrwy ar fy mys,
Fy nynion bychain a dyfon yn fy nghroth.

Mae'n nhw'n ymolchi
Yn lan, yn ymyl y tan,
Fy nynion i.
Dwr o'r bath alcam yn ddu;
Nhw a'u croen wedi cochi.

Rwy'n golchi'u dillad brwnt yn lan
Gyda'm bord a sebon.
Yn sychu'n nhw ar y lein
Ac os ddaw y glaw
Yn ymyl y tan.

Mae'n nhw'n ymadael yn lan,
Fy nynion i.
Y dyn a roddodd fodrwy ar fy mys.
Fy nynion bychain a dyfon yn fy nghroth.

Ann Williams' Song

They come home dirty,
My men.
The man who placed a ring on my finger,
My little men who grew in my womb.

They wash themselves clean
In front of the fire;
My men.
Water from the bath black,
Them with reddened skin.

I wash the dirty clothes clean
With my board and soap,
Drying them on the line.
And, if the rain comes,
In front of the fire.

They leave here clean,
My men.
The man who placed a ring on my finger,
My little men who grew in my womb.

The children of JOHN and ANN WLLIAMS

Lizabeth Ann

Lizabeth Ann, born in Abercanaid in 1888, was John and Ann Williams' first child. Serious, intense, bright and attractive, she went to the local elementary school in Cwmaman where she proved to be an excellent pupil. But, once she was twelve years old, Lizabeth Ann had to leave her studies behind. Staying on at school was not an option for a family with limited means and, anyway, this first-born daughter was needed to help with her younger brothers and sisters. She was good with the little ones and, as a dedicated and devout chapel-goer, she used this flair with children to work as a Sunday-school teacher. In 1914, with the advent of the First World War and most of the young male teachers away, schools were eager to find replacement teachers and formal qualifications weren't always essential. Lizabeth Ann had found her vocation. She eventually married a man much older than herself and the couple had one daughter – Betsi.

It's a pleasure to be in the company of Betsi and her husband, Ted. Their wholesomeness and sincerity shines.

Betsi, severely arthritic, is always cheerful and impressive with her extensive knowledge about Wales and literature – and Cwmaman! Although she remains proudly Welsh-speaking, Betsi worked through the medium of English as a Primary School-teacher in Mountain Ash until her retirement. Her husband, Ted, is a non Welsh speaker, but he shares Betsi's enthusiastic passion for the local chapel, Seion. Between them, the couple have been largely responsible for keeping its doors open in recent years when there has been no Minister. Ted has done much valuable work in the building itself, including restoration and maintenance. Betsi spends her time trying to get hold of people to preach on Sunday, lead services or play the organ. She is single-minded in this respect and perseveres until Seion has its service organised; if she is unable to find the right people, she leads the services herself.

Their devotion doesn't make Betsi and Ted dour. They are lively, have an entertaining sense of humour – and there are few people in Cwmaman who don't know the couple. I visited Cwmaman one evening with my husband recently. We felt that we couldn't leave the village without calling in to see Betsi and Ted and knocked on their door. It was late, they were almost eighty years of age so we crept away quietly, thinking that they'd gone to bed. We later discovered that they had been out caring for an 'elderly' and troubled neighbour.

Lewis John

Lewis John was the oldest son, born in 1890 in Abercanaid. A reserved, kind and thoughtful person, he was little more than a boy when he, in his turn, went down the pit to mine for coal in Cwmaman.

When Lewis John left home to get married, he moved a mile or so away to another village, on the edge of Aberdare, called Aberaman. His wife, SarahAnn, was warm, loving and pleasantly rounded. They remained in the village for the rest of their lives and it was from here, in their little miner's terraced house, that SarahAnn had her two children. Doris was a delicate and sickly child and a source of worry for her parents, who were panic-stricken when the little girl contracted such a severe chest infection that she had difficulty in breathing. SarahAnn held her young child whilst Lewis John ran outside as fast as his legs could carry him. He managed to track down a friend who knew the doctor and the two men rushed up to see if there could be any medical help for the child. Lewis John was not a rich man and doctor's fees were expensive but there is no limit to the efforts made by desperate parents. The doctor duly returned to the house with Lewis John where they found SarahAnn struggling as Doris gasped and wheezed with each breath. The doctor took one look at the three year-old and laid her down flat on the kitchen table. Without wasting any time, he performed an emergency tracheotomy operation.

Doris survived and lived until she was almost ninety. She married, had a daughter and grandchildren.

When Doris was almost grown-up, Lewis John and SarahAnn's second child arrived. Thomas was called Tommie – or just Tom. Sometimes, in life, we meet people who are simply good, kind and warm without a hint of malice, envy or bad temper; Tommie was such a person. As a small child, his sunny personality attracted everybody and there was an almost ethereal quality about him. Tommie was a superb musician and, although he couldn't read music, he could play anything on the piano with professional finesse. His repertoire extended from the latest hits to spirituals – from lengthy classical pieces to the traditional Welsh folk songs. Like his parents, Tommie never left Aberaman. He worked at the local Co-op, married an Aberaman girl and the couple had two children. At one point, he was offered a job entertaining on cruise ships but he turned it down because he didn't want to be separated from his family.

Tommie died too young, in his early fifties. Following a holiday in Spain with his wife, Tommie became ill with a virus. He already suffered from emphysema, the virus infection dehydrated him, and, although he was admitted to hospital, he died before a doctor could attend to him. As was the custom, his body lay at home with all the curtains in the house permanently drawn. There was only one place for Tommie to be – his coffin rested on his beloved grand piano.

Daddy Bom and I often walked down to Aberaman to see Lewis John and his family. Along the dram-road we went, then down past Maes-y-Ffynnon and onto the main road. When we reached the main road, Daddy Bom had to stop for a while to go into a place called 'The Plough'. I was not allowed to go inside – which didn't worry me as it seemed a noisy place. Daddy Bom kept on coming out to see if I was alright, usually with a glass of 'pop' or a packet of crisps for me. Daddy Bom was always in a good mood after being in The Plough and we happily finished our journey.

We were always made welcome in Lewis John's house which smelt of polish, baking and pipe tobacco. Lewis John was gentle and kind and SarahAnn made a fuss of me. I was always fascinated by her name (pronounced SuRAN). I had never heard it before but, when it was written down, I saw that it was just the two names Sarah and Ann linked together.

I was always pleased if Tommie or Dorothy (Doris' daughter) were there. Tommie grinned and smiled at me in such a gentle and kind way that I smiled back. I usually picked wild flowers on our journey over to Aberaman and I gave them to SarahAnn though it was Tommie who called me the 'the flower girl'.

I always wanted him to play the piano and he never refused. I felt like the most important person in the world – he was never too busy doing other things to please me. "What do you want me to play?" he asked, smiling. Sometimes, I could think of a tune and, when I couldn't, he just played, working out from my expression if I liked it. All he wanted to do was to please as he played and played without stopping. It was magical to stand by that piano and see what his hands could do. *Sometimes, they slid gracefully across the keys like elegant ballerinas and, at other times, they seemed to jump up and down – on the black keys and the white ones – finishing by a criss-crossing of his fingers all the way along the instrument from the deep, low notes right up to the high ones at the top. And then his smile spread right across his face. I smiled back at him and he did it all over again just to see me smile.*

When Dorothy came over to play with me, we had a lovely time. My cousin was a couple of months older than me and we were left in the parlour alone for hours on end. The only interruption came from SarahAnn with a tray of cakes or biscuits and glasses of lemonade. Our play centred round the dressing-up box with old clothes, hats, scarves and jewellery; Dorothy and I never tired of our wonderful game. From that little parlour room in Aberaman, we made so many journeys to Hollywood and back – for we were both film stars! If I remember rightly, Dorothy was always Elizabeth Taylor and I was the supporting actress.

Kezziah

There had been a Kezziah in the family for several generations and *this* Kezziah, born in 1894, in Cwmaman, resembled her Biblical namesake. Like the daughter of Job, she was beautiful. This vivacious girl also had her father's lively temperament.

From the beginning, it was clear that Kezziah was a great individualist, unlikely to follow the old pattern of doing some menial work at home until she met a husband who, in all probability, would be a coal-miner. Kezziah was creative, artistic and intuitive. Her gifts found an expression in millinery. With needles and cotton, felt, ribbons, net and feathers, Kezziah created works of art that were exquisite.

At a time when few women moved away except to go into service, Kezziah moved to London. She married an elegant man much older than herself and the couple had one son. The marriage wasn't working – but this situation was usually tolerated by most people. For someone with Kezziah's background, accepting the misery of an unhappy partnership was the usual path. Divorce was expensive so it was only an option for the wealthy but, apart from that, it was against the traditional teachings of the churches and chapels. A divorce was a scandal but that's exactly what Kezziah created. It was the first time that such a thing had happened to anyone in the family.

After the divorce, Kezziah returned to Cwmaman with her son and tried to make peace with the family who had found her so difficult to understand.

Rees

Rees was born in Cwmaman in 1895. He was a bright, intelligent boy but the son of a coal-miner was in no position to have an extended formal education. He went down the coal-mines like his father and brothers. Rees was fired by a strong search for social justice and spent his free-time reading. The mining valleys were well-endowed with libraries, reading-rooms and Institutes to make learning available to every adult – and Cwmaman was no exception. Rees became exceedingly well-read and knowledgeable. His abiding passion was politics. An intense and emotionally-charged man, Rees went out to America for a while but the affluence offended him and he returned to Cwmaman. His wife, Lily Burgess, came from Lancashire and the couple had no children.

Rees' single-minded love of politics and search for social justice was all-consuming and he absorbed all the information he could from newspapers and books. This self-taught man was able to argue and discuss on a level that challenged any University graduate and his political interests led him in a particular direction. Rees was fascinated by the ideals of communism and became a lifelong member of the Party. However he earned a living, Rees' real *mission* in life was to introduce as many people as possible to communism. He sold *The Morning Star* in Aberdare and its surrounding villages then he walked over the mountain to sell it to the residents of Maerdy. Rees was excited when he and a couple of friends managed to book a ticket to go to Russia but his dream of seeing the place was not achieved. He died a few weeks before the departure date.

Even in death, Rees' determination to be true to his ideals, persisted. He had arranged for his body to be left to medical research so there was no funeral for his bereft family. His remains were finally laid to rest in an unmarked, communal plot in a large Cardiff cemetery. His wife, Lil, returned to Lancashire.

Rees and Lil often came to visit my grandparents for tea. At first, they all chatted but it wasn't long before Lil talked to the women in the house and Rees challenged any man present about the state of politics. He used to sit on the little stool beside the fire in the parlour and talk and talk – intense, earnest, a man desperate to be understood and prove his point.

Rees was always kind to me. He stared seriously behind his little round glasses and asked me about school. What subjects did I like? Did I have homework? What did I want to do when I grew up? In spite of all the questions, I never felt nervous with Rees because I could see his eyes move as they listened. They were watching me, they were interested in me and I felt that they cared about me.

Lil seemed very different from Rees. She was a lovely, large lady who always had a powdered nose and she smelt of flowers. She talked almost as much as Rees did but she seemed to be interested in different things.

Blodwen

Blodwen was a tiny girl, born two years before the turn of a new century, in 1898. Even as an adult, she only grew to be about four feet ten inches tall but the size of her personality was huge and immeasurable. Dynamic, funny and emotional, Blod met a local lad from Cwmaman and the couple fell in love. She was only sixteen when the First World War began but they decided to get engaged as her boy-friend volunteered to go out and join the War effort. As everyone thought the War would be short-lived, there was quite a lot of enthusiasm amongst the young men to go out to fight and return as heroes. The enemy had been underestimated, the battle raged for four long years with horrendous numbers of casualties. Blod's fiancé was one of them and she was devastated. Like any other young woman whose dreams had been so cruelly shattered, she grieved and thought that life would never mean much to her again. She thought about what might have been and how it had all been taken away from her. She needed time to mourn. Her fiancé's mother was naturally overwhelmed with grief as well and she found some consolation in Blod's company. The two of them wore their black clothes and talked about the man whom they had both loved and lost.

But Blod was young and, in time, she needed to move on. She was too lively to be dominated by the past. This disappointed her potential mother-in-law and Blod needed to find some escape route. She found an ally in her mother and her mother's family.

Ann Williams was determined that Blod should have the chance for a happier future. Her own sister, Susannah, had emigrated to America and, if Blod could stay with her aunt for a while, she'd be able to see if she liked it over there. If she *did*, she could emigrate and have a new start. Blod went to stay with Auntie Susannah – and she loved America – so she returned to Cwmaman, waited until she was old enough to formally emigrate, said good-bye to her beloved family and sailed off to a new life on the other side of the Atlantic.

The diminutive Blod made her home in Pennsylvania and she soon fell in love again. She was not a classic beauty but her charm and liveliness made her highly attractive. Her husband was a Vice-President of the Bell Telephone Company and they settled in Harrisburg. Blod and Kenneth's lifestyle was unbelievable to the family she'd left behind in Wales. They had a large, detached house with a swimming-pool; later, there was a ranch as well and Blod drove a Buick car. The couple had two sons. One of these sons followed his father's footsteps and became a prominent figure in the Bell Telephone Company. The other son became a lawyer at the White House. Apart from holidays back in Wales, Blod remained in the States for the rest of the life.

There was always great excitement when Auntie Blod came over for a holiday. She needed somewhere to stay and everyone wanted to put her up and catch up with her news. At first, she came over on a ship but, later, she made the journey by plane. This, in itself, was amazing because hardly anyone flew in aeroplanes at the time. I couldn't even imagine what it was like to be above the clouds. I once went to meet her at Gatwick Airport with Daddy Bom and my father and I remember the delight on her face when she first picked us out from the waiting crowd. We were standing behind a kind of iron rail and I wondered why she didn't rush over to us at once. Her smile was so wide that it showed all her teeth but she just waited in a queue with all the other people who'd been on the plane with her. How could she bear that extra wait? At last, she was free and everyone helped her with the luggage which always included boxes full of presents. On every visit, one of those presents was for me. I had a doll that was bigger than any other doll I'd ever seen. If I moved it in a certain way, it made a crying noise that came out from a little area in its back with a circle of tiny holes like a telephone receiver. If it wasn't a doll, it was a dress for me to wear. Again, it was fancier than anything I'd ever seen, with frills and bows and sashes – all in a delicate shade of pink.

Auntie Blod was so different from anyone I knew – just like her presents. To begin with, she had a rich American accent that I'd only ever heard in films. I wondered why she talked like that if she came from Wales. Had she sounded like her brothers and sisters at one time? When did she start to sound like an American? The things Auntie Blod described were also beyond my imagination. She said that she drove her Buick to do the shopping (I never knew why that was so important but all the men in the family said it in such a way that I knew it must be very special). She could park her car, get gas (didn't they use petrol *in America?) and buy everything she needed – food, presents, cards. All this in the one store where she had parked her car! When, years later, I saw my first supermarket in Britain, I began to understand what she meant.*

Auntie Blod was an emotional lady and I remember one occasion when we were walking along a road in Aberdare during one of her visits. I was so interested in her and asked her where her favourite place was. I thought she would say Hollywood or something like that. But she stopped walking and drew in her breath as if she couldn't reply and walk at the same time. I looked at her immaculate made-up face with its red Max Factor lipstick, carefully defined eyebrows and bright green eyelids and saw something beyond it. "My favourite place is Cwmaman!" she said, then, with tears in her eyes, she added "But I could never live there now!"

We looked at each other and I think we had a mutual understanding at a very deep level. Like her, I was living away from Wales and, like her, I knew of a word called hiraeth *that meant so much more than its translation of 'longing for one's country'. I felt very close to her at that moment and asked her what her favourite song was. Again, I expected her to tell me about one of the songs I had heard in some of the American musicals. But, no! With the two of us still standing in the road, lost in time, she said simply, "The Lord's Prayer." We both smiled and carried on walking without saying a word.*

Margaret May (Maggie)

Maggie, the youngest of John and Ann Williams' children, was born in Cwmaman in 1899. Maggie was a robust child and grew up to have many of her mother's physical characteristics. Like Ann, Maggie was short of stature. Like Ann, Maggie was well-rounded. Like Ann, Maggie had an impressively ample bosom. In personality, Maggie resembled her father. She had a loud, strong voice and was dominant and proud. She was not an easy person to argue with or contradict as she spoke with such an air of authority. Maggie, bright and intelligent, married a gentle man called Miles. They settled in the Rhondda town of Porth and had one son who became an Art Teacher.

Empty bottles of Corona fizzy soft drinks used to line up in the passageway of my grandparents' house and when the man called with more full bottles, we had some money off them in exchange for the empties. I loved these drinks – there was American Cream Soda, Dandelion and Burdock and Lemonade.

The main Corona factory was in Porth. I didn't see Auntie Maggie often but, when I did, I realised why everyone called her 'Maggie Bottle of Pop'. She lived by the factory, of course, but she was exactly like the drinks too – fizzy, sparkling and bubbly.

Thomas

Lizabeth Ann, Lewis John, Kezziah, Rees, Blodwen and Maggie had a brother, Tom. Tom, who joined his father and brothers working in the Fforchaman Colliery in Cwmaman, resembled his father physically more than any of his other siblings. With the same dark, swarthy handsome looks, many would have guessed that his native country was somewhere in the Middle East rather than the Valleys of South Wales. Tom was my grandfather – my 'Daddy Bom'.

The last time we spent a holiday together, Daddy Bom and I climbed the Graig Mountain in Aberdare. It was probably not what the doctor advised but we had found gentle ways of getting up to the top along meandering pathways. We reached a point where there were lots of trees and, suddenly, Daddy Bom stopped. He signalled for me to stay where

I was and he went on to 'hide' behind a wide tree-trunk. I knew what was going to happen. He was about to have a coughing bout but I wasn't afraid. I had seen them before. I walked up to him as I watched him cough so badly that he retched. His face changed colour – the grey came first, then the pinkish-red, then purple and, after a while, he turned grey again like a sickly rainbow. He filled his handkerchief as he coughed up the phlegm. I could see blood on it too and, when it was saturated with all the messy gunge, he had to spit on the floor. He leant against the tree-trunk to get his strength back. I held his hand. He looked at me with that beautiful, lovely sad smile.

We carried on climbing and, once we had reached the top, we sat down and looked at the town below us in the Valley. It all looked so tiny – even the high spire of St. Elvan's Church was no bigger than a match-box. We used the church to trace our house then, when we'd found it, I cuddled up to Daddy Bom and tears began streaming down his face. Without saying anything, we both knew that we were very happy just to be there.

JENNET (JINNIE) LEWIS at Aberdare

Jinnie Lewis was a bright young girl with a quick mind and an aptitude for arithmetic. There was no chance of her staying on at school after the age of twelve – especially as her father had died. Her widowed mother, Sarah, wanted to encourage her daughter's gifts but she also needed to find a way to make ends meet. She solved the problem by opening up the parlour of her little home to be a shop which sold sweets and cigarettes. The family lived in the kitchen and the shop did well with its blue-and-white 'Player's Please' tin sign nailed up on the outside wall of the house.

Everybody respected Jinnie, who soon proved to be capable in many other ways than counting out money and weighing two-ounce bags of sweets. Jinnie was good at delivering babies, she

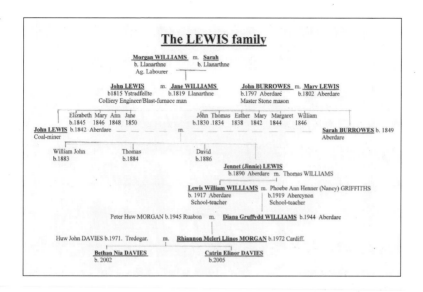

The LEWIS family

Morgan WILLIAMS m. **Sarah**
b. Llanarthne b. Llanarthne
Ag. Labourer

John LEWIS m. **Jane WILLIAMS**   **John BURROWES** m. **Mary LEWIS**
b1815 Ystradfellte b.1819 Llanarthne   b.1797 Aberdare b.1802 Aberdare
Colliery Engineer/Blast-furnace man   Master Stone mason

Elizabeth Mary Ann Jane   John Thomas Esther Mary Margaret William
b.1845 1846 1848 1850   b.1830 .1834 1838 1842 1844 1846

John LEWIS b.1842 Aberdare ‑ ‑ ‑ ‑ ‑ m. ‑ ‑ ‑ ‑ ‑ **Sarah BURROWES** b. 1849
Coal-miner   Aberdare

William John   Thomas   David
b.1883   b.1884   b.1886

Jennet (Jinnie) LEWIS
b.1890 Aberdare m. Thomas WILLIAMS

Lewis William WILLIAMS m. Phoebe Ann Henner (Nancy) GRIFFITHS
b. 1917 Aberdare   b.1919 Abercynon
School-teacher   School-teacher

Peter Huw MORGAN b.1945 Ruabon   m.   **Diana Gruffydd WILLIAMS** b.1944 Aberdare

Huw John DAVIES b.1971. Tredegar.   m.   **Rhiannon Meleri Llinos MORGAN** b.1972 Cardiff.

Bethan Nia DAVIES   **Catrin Elinor DAVIES**
b. 2002   b.2005

Bute Street, Aberdare. Taken at about the time when John and Mary Burrowes lived there. Mid 1800s. (Photograph by kind permission of Aberdare Library)

Sarah Burrowes as a young woman.

Jinnie Lewis (Nana) as a young woman.

Private W. J. LEWIS, son of Mrs Lewis, 4, Elizabeth-street, Aberdare, and brother of Mr T. Lewis, 5, Violet-street, Aberaman, was killed in action on May 9th. He had been in action since the battle of Mons.

Obituary for William John Lewis.

Nana and me. Aberdare 1945.

Holiday in Porthcawl. Tom Williams (Daddy Bom), me, Nancy (my mother), Jinnie Williams (Nana) c. 1952.

was a sensible nurse and she knew how to lay out the dead. Such a woman was a great asset in Aberdare where only the rich could afford doctors. Jinnie brought many babies into the world, dealing successfully with tricky complications such as breech births and twisted umbilical cords.

Thomas Williams had relatives in Aberaman and he used to call in at this sweetshop to buy his cigarettes. He could never go far without a Woodbine or two.

Jinnie was pretty and capable with a keen sense of humour. Tom, with his twinkling eyes, had a mischievous wit and was always ready for a laugh and a shared joke. Over the sale of the Woodbines, the couple got to know each other and the friendship developed into romance. Tom had found the woman he wanted to marry. Jinnie had found the right man. The date was set.

NANA

Jinnie Lewis was my grandmother – my Nana. I could tell that other people thought that Nana was important by the way they spoke to her. There was always a very polite "Good morning, Mrs. Williams!" from everyone – and men raised their hats. Even as a young child, I knew that her job as a school-cleaner was not a good one but everybody seemed to respect her.

Nana was always busy. At home, the fires were attended to all the time and the floors were scrubbed as she went down on her hands and knees to scour away any dirt. Washing was boiled and scrubbed on her washing board with strong-smelling soap before going through the mangle. On a fine day, the clothes were hung on the line or, if it was wet, they were tied up over the fire and all around the kitchen like long, untidy Christmas streamers. It was no place to have secrets! She looked after the tiny garden with devotion and the few square yards of black, black soil always thrived – there was mint for the lamb, other herbs, pom-pom dahlias and gladioli.

I enjoyed going shopping with Nana. At Vaughan's, the Grocer's, Nana had a very regal smile as she asked for her goods. Sometimes it was for two-ounces of meat but she usually asked for "A quarter of roast pork with stuffing please, Mr. Vaughan".

The grocer looked up, smiling, and said, "Your family's down with you then, Mrs. Williams!"

She beamed with pleasure and looked at me with pride. Her family would have nothing but the best! I wondered how much meat Nana and Daddy Bom had when we weren't there?

It took a long time for the meat to reach the standard Nana wanted. Every slice was shown to her on a piece of greaseproof paper after it had been cut. Too much fat and she didn't want it; too much gristle and she wouldn't take it. She refused slices that had too much stuffing or ones where the meat was not a healthy colour. Eventually, the patient Mr. Vaughan checked the weight and asked, "A little over the quarter, Mrs.

Williams, or a little under?" This was another decision for Nana to make and she usually took the extra slice. Then, Mr. Vaughan wrapped the greaseproof paper right round the meat, wrote the weight and price on the outer piece so that Nana knew that she had been fairly charged to the very half-penny – and the prized roast pork went into her basket in a little paper-bag that advertised his shop.

We'd go on then to the market, which was an interesting place with its different stalls and people in search of a bargain. I liked the fruit and vegetable stall best. The lady who sold them was a bit like an apple herself – round and rosy with a cheerful smile. Nana looked at the different apples and touched and smelt them. There were the red apples with their shiny skins, the green ones and others that were a mixture of the two colours. On their skin, the red and green blurred together like an evening sky. It was as if they hadn't decided what colour they wanted to be. I liked the red apples best. At Christmas-time, there were tangerines arranged in a little pyramid. The ones on the top were unwrapped to show off their beautiful colour and the lower ones hid in soft little pieces of tissue-paper that told us where they had come from. How could they have travelled so far across the world to get to Aberdare Market? The bright colour of their skins was so dazzling and foreign that it put the apples to shame – even the red ones. I felt sorry for apples at Christmas.

MORGAN and SARAH WILLIAMS
at Llanarthne

Morgan Williams walked the few miles back home from the cattle market in Carmarthen. Long ago, Owain Glyndwr himself had visited his little village of Llanarthne with its rich, fertile land. Morgan was proud of his little patch of Carmarthenshire but none of it belonged to him. He was just an agricultural labourer and he had mixed feelings about life and the day he'd just spent jostling with the crowd in Carmarthen. However hard he tried, he couldn't help feeling a bit envious of the wealthy landowners with their stock. He'd brought a good herd in himself and received the payment from the drovers who'd taken some of the other cows up to London and Hereford earlier in the year. They had fed them on the rich pasture as they went and, by the time they reached the big English cities, a single fattened cow could fetch five shillings. The drovers seemed to do very well from their trade and so did the farmers. Morgan had the money to hand over to his employer. He, himself, would probably have an extra payment in kind for his efforts – some butter, a little cheese, maybe.

Morgan turned away from his gloomy thoughts and smiled gently to himself. His wife, Sarah, had just given birth to their daughter – they had called her Jane. It was hard to believe that two years had already passed since their wedding on a November day in 1817. Remembering the little one, Morgan hoped that their child would live and grow and thrive. And, as for his dear wife, Sarah, he prayed that she would regain her strength and keep free of infection.

He was almost home when he picked up a few twigs from the pathway. They would help to keep the fire going a little longer – wood was such good fuel! He and Sarah had to rely on anything that was available – and he'd just noticed a few pats of cow dung too! Pleased with himself, he noted the exact spot where the dung lay and hastened his steps. Morgan dropped the money he'd had for the cows into the farm-house, was given a piece of cheese and told the farmer of his discoveries on the road. Then, he left the twigs in their little enclosed garden by the cottage and called in to see Sarah.

"Look!" he said, excitedly, "I've got some cheese, I've found twigs for the fire – and I'm just going back to fetch some cow-dung!" Sarah had little Jane wrapped round her in a blanket and the pair of them were half-asleep. "We'll have some good fires! I won't be long!" he promised.

He took his little wooden cart and shovel and returned to the little heaps. Once the dung was dried, they could use it as fuel too! It didn't last long but, even if it warmed their home for just a couple of hours and enabled Sarah to boil up their pot of supper, it was worth it. The nights were drawing in and he only just managed to pile up his cart before the sun set. Back in the garden, he dumped the dung, picked up the twigs and took them inside.

Sarah and Jane were sleeping. Morgan looked at them tenderly and left them in peace. All would be well and soon Sarah would be taking the baby out with her as she worked. He'd noticed that there was plenty of wool in the hedgerows for her to comb. On a good day, she could fill a whole sack of it. What with the wool and the hemp they'd already gathered from the garden, Sarah would have plenty of spinning to do on winter evenings. He'd already threshed his winter share of corn so they had all they needed to supply them with bread until the springtime. Yes, they had many reasons to count their blessings.

Morgan loved the Spring-time with its promises and it would be good to plough again on a brisk March day. He remembered the first time he saw Sarah on such a day. She followed behind him with the other women, breaking up the surface where the plough had failed. It was strange how a man picks one woman out of all those who are doing the same work. It was Sarah he loved to glimpse as she sowed the seeds, scattering them from left to right from the cloth tied over her shoulder like a sling. Graceful and in rhythm with Nature, she spread the hopes for the Harvest ahead and she would do it again. In no time at all, little Jane – and her brothers and sisters yet to come, would be following their mother, watching her and copying her as she made holes with the dibber for the big swede seeds. They needed to be dropped into the ground, one by one and, once the seeds were settled, Morgan would do what he always had done – he'd spread the thin layer of topsoil that he'd taken away earlier. With all the weeds and insect larvae burnt out of it, it was the best fertiliser anyone could want.

Oh, yes, he was looking forward to the Spring – but, in the meantime, they had the winter to face. He was glad of the cow dung and the twigs. Sarah was awake now – and their little girl was hungry.

JANE WILLIAMS at Llanarthne

Although Jane Williams grew up with her parents and siblings in the heart of the Carmarthenshire country, she saw plenty of people. Llanarthne was so close to the busy market town of Carmarthen that the family often made the journey there on foot, mixing with the drovers and all the folk who were exchanging their cattle and sheep.

Jane helped out in the farmhouse and in the fields. Tending to the animals always took so much time, especially if there was disease or pasture spoilt by bad weather. And then there were the lambs that arrived early when it was still bitterly cold. How hard they all worked to save them! It was always worth the effort, though, and Jane enjoyed sheep-shearing time. She helped to prepare the big meal they all shared at the end of the day but, when she had a moment, she liked to go over to watch the boys in the family. There they'd be, working in pairs, sitting down low on their benches to get the angle right and grabbing hold of each sheep in turn. As soon as they had the animal, they quickly took its legs and tied them together before doing the shearing itself. In no time at all, the fleece was cut away and rolled into a bundle before they seized the next animal. And so it went on until all the sheep had lost their woolly coats! They had to be marked too, the sheep, and their hooves had to be clipped. Jane had stayed long enough and she slipped back to the farmhouse quickly to help the other women – the evening meal would soon be ready!

Farms were spread out in these remote areas so people had to travel some distance to help each other at busy times of the farming year. They walked miles to get to the markets. Amongst these folk were the Lewis family from Ystradfellte who sometimes journeyed over the Black Mountains to the area around Carmarthen. Young John Lewis enjoyed these visits, especially when he found himself attracted to a certain Jane Williams of Llanarthne.

JOHN LEWIS at Ystradfellte

Hundreds and hundreds of years back, when Wales was governed by her own kings and princes, there was a ruler called Hywel Dda (Hywel the Good). 'The Laws of Hywel' had provided a whole series of guidelines for the Welsh people with a great emphasis on family values. One of his laws stated that all sons should have an equal inheritance of their fathers' land. This had worked well for a long time and its fairness avoided all the usual squabbles that can cause such bitter rifts. Eventually, though, the time came when many farms were little more than a few square acres of fields that spread across the country like pieces of patchwork. When English laws were introduced, life became difficult for many people although the wealthier landowners fared well. It didn't take much to ruin small farmers – a few heavy toll charges for a new road or a year of failed crops could be enough to force them to sell up.

John Lewis was born in Ystradfellte in 1815 and he soon became aware of these problems. As a farmer's son, he enjoyed more privileges than most of the other labourers but, as he approached manhood, he knew that life would be grim. His father was still strong and capable and John had two older brothers. There was little chance of him inheriting a decent sized plot of land and he didn't want to stay as a labourer for ever. The work was unbelievably hard and there was little reward. He got plenty of news from the drovers in Carmarthen and they told him about the changes that had taken place in France. It seemed that the ordinary people, who had never had a voice before, had risen up and overthrown the King. As a result, some justice had come to the country, which had a new motto – Liberty! Equality! Fraternity! John wanted some of that! As he owned no land, he couldn't even vote and he saw how members of Parliament just went on representing their area for years and years, completely unchallenged. They were all wealthy landowners who didn't understand the concerns of people. They weren't paid for the job so it was only very rich men who could hope to get into Parliament anyway. Even though there was a spirit of protest beginning to break out in Wales, it would take time to bring about change – and John didn't want to wait until he was an old man to see some improvement in his life. Ystradfellte was a sleepy little place and, though he loved its beautiful setting and its rushing waterfalls as much as anybody, John Lewis needed to earn a living!

He had fallen in love with Jane Williams, a sweet girl from Llanarthne, and they had decided to move away after their wedding. They would discover for themselves what the industries further south could offer them.

JOHN and JANE LEWIS
at Neath and Aberdare

At first, John and Jane Lewis moved a short distance away from their homes to the village of Resolven in the Neath Valley. It was bustling with industry and it was here that their first children were born. But, by 1851, John and Jane Lewis and their family were on the move again and, this time, they travelled further south to the thriving town of Aberdare. This was the town that was to become their permanent home for the rest of their days.

Aberdare was at the height of its wealth and prosperity by the time John and Jane arrived. They had already had time to get used to the busy industrial lifestyle in the Neath Valley – but they took everything in as they looked around their new town. Fiery smoke belched out from the busy ironworks and coal mines marked the landscape everywhere, stretching right across the valley. There were crowds of people around, coming and going from their terraced houses at all times of the day, especially when shifts began or finished in the mines or the furnaces. Others flocked to and from their work on the railways or the canal. And, as for the town itself, it was full of commerce! Apart from the public houses (and there were plenty of those), there were the baker's and butcher's, the fishmonger's and the grocer's, a tea-dealer and a watch and clock-maker…. Anything that they could ever want for themselves and their family was right here in the centre of the town. They admired the new Church of St. Elvan's with its impressively tall spire. Yes, life was going to be good for them here!

John was a capable and intelligent man and he was soon appreciated for his practical skills. There were big networks of rails and drams underground that were needed to bring the coal from the seams to the surface. It took a skilled man to plan and maintain them but it was soon evident that John Lewis possessed the right gifts. He found himself employed as a colliery engineer.

The job enabled him and his family to have better living conditions than they had envisaged and, when he was not working, John enjoyed being at home with his family. The couple lived in Trecynon – a pleasant part of Aberdare – with their five children and a lodger. They often laughed at their foresight in calling their first-born son, John, in 1842. It was good to keep the family names alive and, although Jane went on to have four more children, there would be no other opportunity. Elizabeth had arrived in 1845, followed by Mary, then Ann and the youngest daughter was another Jane!

When he had proved his worth in the coal industry, John Lewis went on to do the same in the Iron Industry, working as a blast-furnace man. Making iron was a long and tricky process and John wasn't involved in the earliest stages when the ore was blasted out of its narrow seams and crushed or when local coal was roasted in kilns to make coke. John's job began when he helped to load the coke and iron ore with the untreated limestone into the top of the blast-furnace. Here, as it was fuelled by blasts of air – some hot, some cold – the material made its way down to the bottom of the furnace. After several hours, the molten iron was hot enough to leave the base of the furnace and it fell out as rods into the pig beds in the sand underneath.

"Are there real pigs sleeping at the furnace, Daddy?" the children had asked.

"No!" chuckled John.

"Then why do they call them 'pig beds'?"

It was a good question as children's enquiries usually are.

John explained patiently. "When the hot iron comes out at the bottom, the heat has made it a different shape," he began. "It's bent and someone said that it looks like a sow suckling her little ones!"

"Ah!"

It was funny how things got their names! Some of the pig iron was refined again to become cast iron but, by this time, John's part in the process was over. He didn't have an easy job and the furnace wasn't called a furnace for nothing – the heat was unbearable. The work was hard on the eyes and it was so easy to get burnt but it paid well and he was able to take five pounds and nine shillings home every month.

By this time, his one and only son – named after him – was already proving his worth. Young John Lewis had been working as an errand-boy since the age of nine. He was certainly kept busy for there were plenty of errands to be run in such a busy town as Aberdare!

JOHN LEWIS in Aberdare

When little John Lewis was running errands in Aberdare in 1851, the town was turning out about 500,000 tons of coal a year. It was not surprising that he soon left his childhood job to join the thousands of other people who were working down in the mines.

Shifts were long but John got used to them. By the time he'd made the journey to and from work and had a bath, fifteen hours of the day had gone. Things could be worse and it was a great comfort to be home at night with hot water from the kettle poured into the zinc bath. John rubbed the coal-dust off as best as he could and his mother was there to help him with the parts of his back that he couldn't reach. She often brought cold compresses for his eyes too. When coal or grit had fallen into them during the day, there was never enough light to attend to them so they were often burning and sore by the time he came home. The warm water soothed his body too, after all the hours on his knees or lying on his side. Refreshed, John was just thankful that he hadn't been seriously injured and he was more than ready to tuck into his evening meal.

His mother, Jane, took good care of him but, before long, it was a wife who poured the hot water from the kettle into his bath. John married a local girl and, if life was tough on him underground, he knew that women had their own hardships too. As a child, he had been surrounded by four sisters so he had some inkling of their worries. There were times when they felt faint and tired and, from the moment a woman felt a new baby inside her, there could be so many problems. Even when all went well, the little ones didn't always survive. There were terrible diseases and no doctors. And the new mothers themselves came down with fevers and infections. John hoped that his young wife would be fortunate. He was disappointed – she was another woman to die early of a woman's lot.

Naturally, John grieved for her but no wishful thinking would bring her back. He needed someone else to support him. It was so hard to come home from work, black and exhausted, with no woman in the house to care for him and share the events of the day. There were enough women in the family to ensure that his children were cared for – but he needed another wife. John began courting Sarah Burrowes – a young woman from Aberdare. They needed time to be sure of each other but the day came when John asked Sarah's father for her hand in marriage.

JOHN and MARY BURROWES at Aberdare

In 1875, John Burrowes was an old man. He had seen so much in his long life but he wanted to be assured of one final thing. His youngest daughter, Sarah, was still unmarried and he hoped that he'd live to see her settled. He wanted to give her away in marriage to a good man. He was very proud to do exactly that when he walked with her to Siloa Chapel. His beloved daughter had entered the building on his own arm as Miss Sarah Burrowes. She left it as Mrs. John Lewis.

John Burrowes was born in Aberdare a few years before the turn of the nineteenth century. As a small child in 1800, he knew an Aberdare that was nothing more than a village with lush corn-fields, hidden from the outside world by its splendid oak trees. The land was rich enough to provide all the food required locally so there was no need to travel. This was just as well because the road tracks were dusty and no-one had any means of transport but horseback – or their own two feet! It was a farming community whose people were used to a simple life. There were good harvests and there were bad harvests; there was kind weather and there was cruel weather. The men worked in the fields, the women had the children and cooked oatmeal bread, root vegetables and salted bacon. If things were going well, the families would enjoy butter, cheese and fruit too. One generation followed another in the way they had done for centuries.

However, as John Burrowes grew into manhood, everything changed. The village became a town and it seemed to be growing bigger every day. Aberdare was rich in iron and coal and, suddenly, these industries grew to such an extent that the old place was unrecognisable. Land was taken up with the collieries and Ironworks themselves – and the men who worked in them needed homes, too. Terraced houses were built quickly to accommodate them and their families. As soon as another row had been finished, news came that even more men were needed as another Colliery or Ironworks was opened. This growth spiralled with an almost unbelievable speed until there were houses stretching right across the Valley. There were thousands of them, little stone dwellings, packed closely together, back to back. Every inch seemed to be filled with them – and they even reached the edge of the mountains.

John Burrowes didn't join the thousands of other local men who went to work with coal or iron. As Aberdare grew, the new influx of workers and their employers needed craftsmen. John became apprenticed to a stone-mason as a journeyman. He was kept very busy because most people needed to call upon the services of a mason at some time in their lives. It was a tough, dusty job that needed strong hands, firm muscles and a team of helpers. There was so much that had to be done! In the early years, John worked for other men but he hoped the time would come when he'd be employing men to work for *him*. Maybe, in due course, his own sons would follow in his footsteps and they could establish a family business! That was something for the future but, in the meantime, he had to be content with starting on the lowest rung of the ladder. He was given some of the simplest – and heaviest – tasks. Firstly, the stone had to be extracted – and that was a long and dirty job in itself. Then, it had to be checked for quality – good-looking stone sometimes had weaknesses and there was no point dragging it around if it was unsuitable for the work. When the stone had been hauled to his employer, John watched as the experienced mason chiselled away at the big, formless chunks, shaping them and polishing. When the stone was finally ready, it made its journey to the customer – and it was often John who delivered it.

John Burrowes married and the couple had children. Unfortunately, his wife was another poor woman to fall victim to the scourge of disease and infection. When she died, John grieved but life had to move on. He married for the second time and his new bride was another Aberdare woman – Mary Lewis.

John and Mary settled into their house in Bute Street, right in the heart of the town. Mary produced a large family and, by 1841, she and John had seven children – John, Thomas, Mary, Esther, Margaret, William and the baby of the family – little Sarah. John had dreamt about a family concern and he saw that becoming a reality. He was now a skilled master stone-mason in his own right and employed his two oldest sons, John and Thomas, as his journeymen.

Mary Burrowes was a strong woman who survived all her pregnancies but life at home was a struggle. She tried very hard to keep her little house clean but it wasn't easy. In such a built-up area, she and her neighbours had to pour out their buckets of waste onto the road outside. It was easier when Aberdare had been a rural village but now, with so many people living close together, the stench became very bad as the waste mingled with the rainwater that trickled down from the mountain. There were no drains and the whole smelly mess ran down the streets and spilt over into the river. No-one seemed to have any answers to these problems but, then, in 1849, something happened to put John and Mary in fear of their own and their children's lives. John heard about it at work and Mary talked about it with the neighbours.

"There's disease spreading round Aberdare!" The women's voices were hushed as they spoke on their door-steps. "People are dying!"

"What can we do to stop it? Is it something bad in the air?"

"No-one knows!"

"What's its name?" Mary asked.

The reply was whispered.

"Its name is cholera!"

The epidemic passed and John and Mary Burrowes were so thankful that their family had been spared from its clutches. Most of the children were grown up by this time and leading their own lives. John was getting old now and he and Mary talked about the things that were important to them. He had worked hard and enjoyed having his sons helping him. He was grateful to Mary for her loyalty and the children she had borne him. They had a roof over their head and they had survived the cholera epidemic. They had their faith. John knew that he was probably nearing the end of his life and was delighted to see Sarah, their youngest child, in her bridal gown. All would be well!

JOHN LEWIS and SARAH BURROWES
at Aberdare

"Here they are!" Sarah Burrowes called out excitedly to her family. "Here they are! Here they are!"

It was 1873 and they had joined the crowds in Aberdare who had turned out to welcome the heroes home. Everyone began applauding and craning their necks to get a better glimpse.

"There's Caradog!" Sarah smiled as she caught sight of the great man himself.

Aberdare was aflame with pride and joy that day; sweet singing filled the air. The people of London now knew about their town! It was famous – thanks to Caradog and Y Cor Mawr (The Big Choir).

Caradog's real name was Griffith Rhys Jones. He was a local blacksmith and a musical conductor who had helped to build up a huge choir of five hundred local people. Under his baton, they had practised and practised until their voices seemed to be coming from Heaven itself. And then, they had all gone up to London – to Crystal Palace – to compete with the best choirs from all over England and Wales. News had come that they had done very well – *so* well, in fact, that they had won first prize. And here they were at last, home, triumphant! They had proved to the whole country that there was more to Aberdare than coal. The clapping continued – no-one wanted to let them go!

The memory of that happy day boosted the morale of the whole town. Sarah married the man she loved – John Lewis – two years later, and that pride helped the couple to be positive about everything. Yes, John had to face dangers every day in his work underground – but they were no strangers to such problems. They would overcome them! John's first wife had died but Sarah would take good care of him. They'd work together to build up a happy home life. Change was slow in coming to the mines but things were getting better. Yes, there were still accidents underground – but there were better safety measures now. Some of the old injustices were being put right. John and Sarah were resilient and, however life treated them, they would manage!

They went to live in a miner's terraced house in Aberaman, a village on the edge of Aberdare. John continued hacking away at the coalface and Sarah washed his clothes, cooked his meals and helped him as he took the evening bath in front of the coal fire. The home was seldom empty. Sarah had step-children to see to until they were old enough to make their own lives and, when she married John, she had gained four sisters-in-law. As for John, he now had six brothers and sisters-in-law.

Sarah was a good, hard-working wife. Every morning, she went out onto her front door step with an empty jug, waiting for the milkman to come closer to her house with his horse and cart so that she could have her daily supply. As the man emptied some of the milk from the churn into his 'jack' to make sure that he was giving the right amount, Sarah held her jug out for him when it came to her turn. Her hand was firm – she couldn't allow a single drop of the precious, white food to be spilt or wasted. When she had her fill, Sarah paid him, wished the man good day and listened as he went on to the next batch of houses. The horse's gait made the churns rattle and the noise brought another group of women to their front doors.

This was the time when Sarah stopped for a moment to chat with her neighbours and catch up on any news. Conditions in the mines were always topics of conversation and no-one talked about anything else if there had been an accident or an explosion. They were all ready to rally round and help a family if a man had been hurt. Sarah enquired about any neighbours who were ill and the women discussed the different ways of treating their ailments. They talked about the shops and the price of goods. They complained if the rainy weather was preventing them from drying the clothes – and they talked about their children! Many of the women had their little ones clinging onto their long skirts and Sarah smiled at them before taking her milk supply inside. It went straight into the cupboard and, because it was summer-time, she put the jug in a bowl of cold water to keep it cool and fresh. However, as she attended to the rest of her morning's work, there was a sadness in Sarah Lewis' heart that she kept from her neighbours. Unlike them, she didn't have a baby wrapped in a shawl, crying and needing the breast. Unlike them, she didn't have a toddler to wean onto the milk from the jug in the cupboard.

Sarah had to wait eight long years before she had her own baby. William John was born in 1883 and then she went on to have three more children fairly quickly. Thomas was born the following year, a third son, David, arrived two years later and, to complete the family, a daughter, Jennet (known as Jinnie), was born in 1890.

John and Sarah had to abide by the new law that made it compulsory for all children to go to school until they were twelve years of age. Everyone found this difficult because children as young as five had always been a source of a small extra income. But maybe the education would make some difference? Whatever the boys managed to learn at school, it wasn't long before they followed their father down in the mines. Their young, supple bodies knew how to bend and creep into the narrowest of spaces underground and John was proud of them. He kept an eye on his sons and, although their small income went to him – the father, no-one minded because Sarah was determined that all the family would be well cared for. They were managing as well as anyone else in the same position but they didn't expect the big blow that was about to hit them. John Lewis died in 1899.

In the midst of her grief, Sarah had to think quickly about the future. Thankfully, the boys were working – William John was already sixteen, Thomas was fifteen and even Davie, the youngest son, was thirteen. But although there was no financial crisis in the immediate future, Sarah knew all too well that, when they were ready to marry, her sons would leave home and have to provide for their own wives. And what about her only daughter, Jinnie – their bright little girl who was only nine years old when she lost her father? What would happen to them in three years' time when Jinnie left school and the boys were thinking of moving out? Jinnie was doing very well at school – her teachers said that she was very good at arithmetic – so Sarah decided that she would use her daughter's gifts in a way that would earn them a little money. The house in Aberaman had the usual two rooms downstairs but the parlour was only used 'for best'. They could manage by living in the kitchen and the front parlour could be made into a shop. All they needed were some weighing-scales, a basic stock of goods, sweet jars, a little counter – and they were in business! They'd work hard so that the newest commercial enterprise in Aberaman would be a success. They would survive!

Just as Sarah and her family were adjusting financially and emotionally to life without John, another blow hit the family. This time, it was a shock for the whole of the country. In August 1914, they heard that Britain was at War with Germany. Sarah shuddered. It was not a good time to have young adult sons.

The children of JOHN and SARAH LEWIS

William John Lewis

William John left his childhood home, got married and had children. They remained in Aberdare but, when the Great War began, he decided to sign up. He was twenty-nine years old when he said goodbye to his wife, his five young children and his widowed mother but he was convinced that the separation would be a short one. He was initially caught up in the Battle of Mons and stayed on as the fighting grew bloodier. It was tougher than he had expected but surely it had to end soon. This was a different kind of war with heavy cannons and trucks and tanks instead of the horse-backed soldiers of old. Britain had many allies and the Empire to back it. Yes, hostilities would be short-lived and he'd be back with his precious family for Christmas!

But the War brought huge casualties and it was *not* swift to end. Day after day, there was bad news. Every family seemed to have lost at least one member and some lost an entire generation of their men. Sarah Lewis waited. William John's wife waited. The dreaded telegram came and the news was not good. William John, Sarah's beloved first-born son, had been killed in action. He was an honest young man who had responded to Kitchener's posters that pointed the finger to touch the conscience. He had wanted to fight so that the country would be free and a safe place for his children. Now, he had gone for ever, leaving behind a widow and five young fatherless children. Although William John was just *one* official casualty, the lives of many others had been shattered. In the unnumbered toll of suffering that comes with each death, there was the brokenness of his wife, his five children, his mother, sister and brothers. Such is the legacy of war.

After her tragic loss, William John's widow did not live long herself and, on her death, there were five orphans. Jenny, Cliff, Rachel (Ray), May and Elizabeth had no home and no money to support them. In a desperate bid to keep the family together, William John's sister, Jinnie, offered to bring them up herself. Jinnie was married by this time and living in a miner's terraced house in Aberdare with her husband and her mother, Sarah. Although her home had just two rooms downstairs and two upstairs for its three inhabitants, it had not been unusual for a house of that size to hold up to fourteen people. But Aberdare was in the process of changing its rules and regulations in the interests of public health. The town, like so many others in the Industrial areas, had been victim to epidemics of dreadful diseases and they were forced to do something about the overcrowding and lack of sanitation. Because of this, Jinnie's warm invitation of a home for her nephew and nieces was not accepted. The only alternative was for them to be brought up in a local church orphanage. None of them thrived there. They all left the institution as soon as they could. The girls did the most popular thing at the time – they all went into service in London. Jenny, Ray, May and Elizabeth – the girls who had missed out on so much parental love themselves, went to work caring for the needs of the rich. One of the advantages of this escape-route was that it provided further opportunities for the future. They all moved on to train as nurses. Sadly, Elizabeth didn't live long enough to benefit – she died at the age of twenty. Jenny was the most successful of all the girls, becoming a nursing sister in one of the famous London hospitals. Ray remained a spinster and May and Jenny married in middle-age. Neither of them had children and May died a few years after her wedding.

Cliff was William John's only son and he ventured further afield than London. As soon as he was old enough and could afford the fare, Cliff emigrated to Canada. He wanted a complete escape. He settled down there, found work and married – but his happiness was short-lived. One day, their house in Canada went up in flames. Cliff and his wife, Ethel, managed to get out of the smoke-filled rooms alive but then Cliff realised that his mother-in-law was still trapped inside. Instinctively, he ran back into the blaze to save her. They were both found, burnt to death, in each other's arms.

Cliff and his wife had no children.

★

Sarah Lewis had the painful experience of losing her oldest son and his wife and then seeing their children – her grandchildren – forced into an Orphanage. Sarah herself lived into her eighties, long enough to see a Cenotaph erected in Aberdare in 1923 to honour the hundreds of Aberdare men who had lost their lives in the Great War. Maybe this offered some consolation.

When Sarah eventually died, the family ensured that her life was honoured. A crowd gathered in the house in Elizabeth Street, Aberdare. The women were dressed in long black coats and hats with mourning veils and, just before the funeral cortege set off, her daughter, Jinnie, gathered all the children together to see the proceedings from outside. The hearse that carried Sarah's body arrived in a beautiful glass coach drawn by two fine black horses with coats like silk. The children had never seen anything like it and they watched as the coach took Sarah away from her home for the last time, followed by a long procession of men who kept her company to the cemetery.

A Oes Heddwch Nawr?
Cri Sarah Lewis

Fy mab cyntafanedig
Tyfodd ei esgyrn a'i gnawd
Yn fy ngroth.

Yr un esgyrn a chnawd,
Sy'n nawr yn pwdru
Ar bridd estron.

Dy Fab Uniganedig
Twyna'r ddaear
Ac anwesu fe.

Is There Peace Now?
The Cry Of Sarah Lewis

My first-born son.
His bones and flesh
Grew in my womb.

The same bones and flesh
That now decay
On foreign soil.

May Your only-begotten Son
Warm the earth
And cradle him.

I remember May, Jenny and Ray though I didn't see them often. May was a sweet, coy woman who smiled and laughed in the way people do when they are shy and gentle. I have the vaguest recollection of Ray but I recall Jenny coming down to Nana's house just after she married. I was surprised that she was such an old bride; she had some grey in her hair. Her husband was a quiet, smiling man and Jenny asked me if I liked him. The question worried me because her new husband was standing right in front of me, still smiling. It seemed odd that she was asking me! What could I say? I looked at the happy man and I noticed Jenny's face. She wanted me to say 'Yes' – so I did. Her husband's grin grew even wider and Jenny put a hand on my shoulder as if to say' Thank you'.

In Nana's house, all the food came in fresh from the market, the grocer or the butcher. There was never much left at the end of the day but anything that did *remain was kept in the white cupboard in the parlour. The cupboard had a door to keep the food cool – this was usually meat – and it was also the place where pickles were kept. One day, I noticed several jars in the corner of the cupboard and I asked Nana what they were. She didn't want to show me at first but I persevered and she brought one of the jars out for me to see. The label said 'Maple Syrup. Produce of Canada'. I asked her what maple syrup was and she didn't seem to know. Why was she keeping jars of things when she didn't know what they were? I liked syrup and treacle tarts – could this syrup be used in pies?*

Many years later, I discovered the truth. Ethel, Cliff's widow, sent Nana a jar of maple syrup every year at Christmas. It was her way of keeping in touch with the woman who had offered hospitality to her Cliff and his sisters. Nana didn't know what maple syrup was for and I think that the jars remained unopened.

Thomas Lewis

In most families, there are rifts. For some reason, Jinnie and her brother, Thomas, had fallen out and, as a result, I never got to know him. I met him twice – once, at the swimming baths in Aberdare when Nana and her brother had a strained and awkward conversation. The other occasion was at Nana's funeral. The rift softened in the face of death.

David Lewis

David was a handsome young man and the third son of John and Sarah Lewis. He went down to work in the mines as a collier in the Fforchaman Colliery at Cwmaman (the same colliery where his brother-in-law, Thomas, worked). As a miner, he was exempt from War service but he paid a high price for his labour. Davie was seriously injured underground. He lost an eye and, following the accident, worked as a store-man. He married a local girl, Maggie, and the couple remained in Aberdare with their two daughters.

I remember Uncle Davie and his family well.

Nana was very close to Davie and went up to spend one evening a week at his home. If I was down in Aberdare, I went with her. We used to go there early in the evening, up the streets and across, quick as squirrels, and over to Monk Street where I had a good view of the mountain. This was my mountain – the Graig! I loved it as much as a real person and watched as the buses zig-zagged their way down over the bendy, steep road from Maerdy. We stopped at Monk Street to go into the Fish and Chip shop which Nana said was one of the cleanest in the town. There, we watched as buckets of white, sliced potatoes were poured into the sizzling fat and Nana chatted away as the huge frying pan was lifted from time to time to see if the chips were brown enough. If they weren't ready, down they went again! The fish was usually in a little closed case on top of the frying-areas with a clear front so that everybody could see them and point out their chosen fish. The word 'hake' was said as if it was something very special and Nana chose a fillet for me which rested in a paper bag on newspaper until the eagerly-awaited chips were ready. Salt was generously shaken all over the food and a few little balls of batter that had come free of the fish were added for my benefit. They were delicious and second only to the chips as my favourite food. I had the hake mainly to please Nana. Then, we walked the rest of the way to Uncle Davie's house where I began to eat my lovely supper. The newspaper had turned dark and oily by this time and, although I was offered a plate, I preferred to eat them straight out of the newspaper. These were tastes that made me feel happy and contented and the newspaper and the smell were all part of the experience. I don't think I ever left anything but the fish skin.

By the time I had finished eating, Nana and Davie were deep in conversation in their chairs by the fire. Auntie Maggie usually left the two of them to chat, coming up to us from time to time with a cup of tea or a glass of pop. I didn't understand most of the conversation but I picked up the moods. Some words were very serious and unhappy – these were about 'the dust' and 'compo money' and 'disease'. There were also happy words. 'Porthcawl' was a happy word and I knew why. Porthcawl was the place where everyone went on holiday and there was nothing there but sand, high tides, donkey rides, a fun-fair and sunshine.

When I got tired of listening, I looked round the room. I liked to watch the fire because that, too, could be happy or sad. It was sad when it burnt down and still sad for a while after the new coal had been put on it. Then it became cheerful and warm and there were all sorts of shapes in the flames that changed colour and made patterns. Some of these were just pretty like something in a kaleidoscope but sometimes I could see things that I recognised there – a witch or a dragon or a mountain. The wallpaper was another thing that made patterns. Again, some of them were just interesting but, at other times, I could make out peoples' faces. There were silhouettes or eyes on their own with a swirl of hair.

Another thing I noticed was Uncle Davie's eyes. I had been told that it was rude to stare but I couldn't stop myself. Both eyes were dark and shining but only one of them moved – so it was hard to know where he was looking. Which one was the 'pretend' eye? How was it fixed? Did it hurt? Could you take it out? If you could take it out, what was underneath? These were questions I only dared to ask myself.

I got to know Auntie Maggie – who always had a smile for me – and her two daughters, Gwendo and Margery. Gwendo – the older daughter, was married and the family was always pleasant to me. I played with her three children. The youngest of these – Janet – had been delivered by Nana herself.

Margery was much younger than her sister and her life seemed very glamorous to me. She was married to a large, tall man with a generous laugh and the two of them were very happy though they had no children. Margery was a hairdresser and she became the manageress of her own salon before lecturing in the subject at a local college. She and Bill had the chance of a lifetime when a titled family with Royal connections needed a husband-and-wife team to act as coiffeuse and chauffeur. With their new, regal address, the couple travelled around to the most interesting of places.

Margery and Bill were the first people in the family to travel abroad. They had just come back from a place called Majorca when we saw them in Aberdare. Margery told of sunshine that I couldn't even imagine and, to prove that she was telling the truth, she removed her wedding-ring. That little patch of her finger had a different kind of ring – a white one made from flesh that stood out in contrast to the rest of her fingers and hands. She showed us her 'tan' (a new word for me, which meant 'going brown in the sun'). I had never seen anything like it in my life!

THE EXTENDED FAMILY

Nana's large family had lived in Aberdare for several generations. Her father and one of her grandfathers had been married twice so there were countless relatives who came to her house and, for the most part, I was never really clear about their exact link.

Katie Kangaroo often came to tea. I have no idea why she had this name (which was never used to her face). I don't think she came from Australia and I only saw her in the house so I don't know if she walked with huge strides. She wore a camel coat so why wasn't she called Katie Camel?

We often went to see Peggy Pontypridd (there was no problem with understanding how she got her name). In Ponty, we usually browsed around the market first which was even more exciting than the one in Aberdare. Men selling cloth threw the rolls into the air so that, when they caught them again, some of the cloth was loosened. They stroked it then as if they were in love before trying to get their audience to buy. After the Market, we went on to see Peggy − a sweet woman, who worked in a shop that sold underwear. As the grown-ups talked, I wandered up and down the aisles, observing the secret world of those hidden clothes for men, women and children. Some liberty bodices were bought for me − those lovely, comforting garments that I wore over a vest in the winter.

Another group of relatives often came on the bus from Maesteg. One day, there were three generations of them, including my little cousin who was several years younger than me. She had been violently sick on the bus and everybody made a great fuss of her. She was given cups of sweet tea, had to sit by the fire not to get a chill and was relieved of her clothes so that the vomit could be rinsed off. The little girl had a greyish-white face and looked shaken and very unwell. As she sat silently, she was given some of my clothes to wear until hers were dry. They didn't fit her. I didn't know what to say to her so I smiled. She smiled back. The whole house smelt of sick which made me feel sick and, although I felt very sorry for my cousin, all I wanted was for the house to smell normal again. I used a trick that I had just discovered. It involved smiling even though bad thoughts were going on inside my head. I had believed that other people (especially grown-ups) could tell what I was thinking. In between the fussing, there was great interest expressed in my cousin's beautifully permanently pleated skirt. Would it lose its pleats and shape after all the sponging and washing? If it didn't, it was indeed a miracle. The skirt was clean and dry for the journey home and her pleats remained a permanent feature.

DEAR OLD PALS

Inevitably, in such close communities, friendships were formed that stood the test of time. They created a whole set of 'honorary' aunts, uncles and cousins.

My grandparents, Jinnie and Tom Williams, were great pals with Joe and Annie. Joe, a local cobbler, died early but Jinnie, Tom and Annie retained a close bond which passed down through several generations. Lew (Tom and Jinnie's son) and Iris (Annie and Joe's daughter) were about the same age and they were inseparable.

When they were in good form, Jinnie and Annie were very entertaining, recalling stories of their escapades and reciting long Victorian ballads such as 'Little Nell' by heart. These performances showed talent worthy of drama school.

Iris and Lew were bosom pals who always defended each other. The first time Iris saw Lew playing on the rugby field, she witnessed him being tackled and ran onto the field with her umbrella, ready to hit the boy who had been wicked enough to hurt her Lew!

Lew and Iris were as close as any brother and sister, and remained so after marriage. Iris' new husband, David, was away with the Navy in the Second World War and the couple had little chance to spend any time together. Everyone stopped what they were doing to listen to the wireless at six in the evening for any special announcements. News broke about some casualties at sea and their names were given out on the air. David was one of them. Some time later, Iris married a good-natured Cockney called Stan.

Iris and Stan had many parties in their house and they were always good fun. I spent half the time in the back room with Nana and Auntie Annie and the other half in the front-room where there was singing and a tuneful piano.

Nana and Auntie Annie were fond of recounting stories. I often heard one of their favourite tales. The two women had been to the Rex cinema on their own (quite a daring thing to do in those days!) When the film was over, they met a man in the foyer who was very distressed. They asked him what the problem was and he told them how hard his life was and how he had been left to fend for himself after countless personal disasters. He was frightened to go home on his own over the mountain road back to Maerdy. Jinnie and Annie – Good Samaritans that they were – decided to escort him home. As they climbed the Graig mountain and walked down towards Maerdy, the man continued telling them his tale of woe and the two women sympathised. However, as they approached his lonely home, there was a woman standing on the door-step. She was his wife – and she was very angry. Jinnie and Annie scuttled away hastily to face the mountain road back on their own. By this time, it was pitch-dark. On a very isolated part of the mountain, they heard heavy breathing and were too frightened to move. Who was this mystery person so close to them? No-one would hear them if they were in trouble. What was going to happen to them? When they told the story, Nana and Auntie Annie strung it out for all that it was worth. The 'deep breather' was a wild mountain horse! Jinnie and Annie were two formidable ladies – and they might have frightened the horse!

In the front room, Stan played the piano as he and my father sang. The songs were always the same – 'Hear My Song, Violetta', 'Santa Lucia', 'Come Back to Sorrento', and 'The Whiffenpoof Song'. Beer glasses were filled and re-filled and the singing improved.

Iris and my mother, Nancy, didn't have good singing voices but they always did a 'turn'. They usually disappeared upstairs, dressed themselves up in anything that was a bit flouncy and came downstairs, dancing the can-can and shouting 'Follow, follow, the merry, merry pipes of Pan!' They didn't keep this up long as they both dissolved into hysterical laughter.

Shy though I was, I, too, had my party-piece. Standing by the piano, I sang a song all about a young queen in a golden coach. Everybody clapped!

One of the most entertaining and interesting of these 'relatives' was Iris' cousin, Gwyneth. She was one of those people who, completely untrained, had a true, powerful singing voice: she could also take hold of any instrument and play it by ear within seconds. I loved Gwyneth and was amazed that she was so cheerful. Her only daughter, Dorothy, had died as a young girl. During her illness, Dorothy had received visions and told people all about what Jesus was saying to her. She told some relatives who had argued that Jesus wanted them to make their peace with one another before she went to live with Him. The rift was healed. Dorothy died. After her death, Gwyneth's grief response was to enter wholeheartedly into life. She had a great gift with children (including me and my daughter) and seemed to bear no bitterness about her own loss. When she was much older and widowed, Gwyneth listened to the radio at night when she felt lonely. On one such occasion, she fell asleep and woke to hear angelic voices. 'Daro, that was easy!' she said to herself. For a few moments, Gwyn thought that she had died and gone to Heaven. Reality sunk in and she lived to tell the tale with great humour.

NANA and DADDY BOM

Tom and Jinnie Williams married in the year that saw the beginning of the First World War. They went to live in a terraced house in the heart of Aberdare and, a few years later, Jinnie's widowed mother, Sarah, joined them. Tom continued to work down in the mines so he was exempt from active service. Jinnie's offer to bring up her orphaned nephew and nieces was rejected but there was soon a child of her own to rock. When Tom and Jinnie's son was born in 1917, he was given the family names of

Lewis and William. It was evident from the beginning that the child was not only handsome but highly intelligent. However difficult their own lives were, they were determined that Lew would be given the chance to escape from the vicious circle of poverty into which they had always been locked.

Tom walked along the dram-road every day to and from work in the Fforchaman Colliery in Cwmaman and returned in the evenings, exhausted. Jinnie had to look after her son, her ageing mother and keep the house. When Tom's shift was over, she brought in the tin bath that hung from a hook in a small area outside the back-door with the scrubbing-board and mangle. In front of the fire, she poured in some cold water before adding the boiling water from the kettle. Tom soaked himself, rubbing his skin with the strong soap until the coal dust had gone. As he stepped out to dress again by the fire, Jinnie carried the bathwater away. Water was precious but the dirty water was too black to be used for much so she poured it onto her little garden. There was the washing to do and the drying and the airing. She had a flat iron that was heated on the fire and used to press the garments. All the floors had to be scrubbed and everything was spotlessly clean. No-one would guess that a miner covered in coal dust came near the place.

Lew was still getting good reports at school and Jinnie, in particular, forced him to do all the homework he could. If he passed the scholarship when he was eleven, he'd be entitled to go to the Grammar School. Jinnie had left school herself at the age of twelve but she became her son's informal home tutor in the evenings as she tested him on all his work – and made him repeat anything that was not perfect. Her efforts paid off! Lew passed the scholarship examination and Tom and Jinnie proudly signed the piece of paper from the Education Committee to confirm that they would support him in his studies until the age of sixteen. Looking at the curriculum, it was hard for them to believe that their own son was to have the privilege of learning so many things. Lewis William Williams was the first person in the family to have such an education and their pride overflowed when he went on to win a scholarship place in Southampton University to read Mathematics.

The books were bought and Lew made the journey to Southampton but, just as he was about to begin his studies, he received notice that his father, Tom, was now so ill that the family needed him back home. Lew was overwhelmingly disappointed and Jinnie was devastated. Tom felt ashamed.

Tom's health continued to cause grave problems over the years and the struggle with the Authorities added insult to injury. Pneumoconiosis was an occupational disease and there was the thorny problem of compensation money. Tom had been a miner since the age of twelve. By the time he was thirty, he was made redundant because of the eye condition that he had contracted from his work underground. After several years of light employment, Tom returned to work as a Labourer at Tower Washery and this was followed by a stint as an assistant sawyer. By 1950, he was unable to do any work at all.

These periods of light employment (or no employment at all) meant that the family was in dire straights. If Lew would *ever* be able to get another chance to continue his education in the future, this would only be possible if Jinnie went out to work as the sole bread-winner herself. Tom underwent examination after examination for different Boards and Panels and had to see a number of doctors in the process. Their diagnoses varied considerably. One surprising observation noted that the 'nystagmus' was a psychoneurosis. Other opinions varied although the diagnosis of pneumoconiosis was confirmed several times. Someone mentioned carcinoma of the lung but in the autumn of 1955, it was felt that the pneumoconiosis had not deteriorated. A month later, Thomas Williams was dead. The oxygen cylinders that had been by his bed in the parlour had finally failed to help him. Pneumoconiosis did not feature on the death certificate so Jinnie was not entitled to any compensation money at all. Her only concession was the ton of coal that was dumped in front of the house free of charge. She carried it back through the house to the coal-shed, bucket by bucket, saving even the dusty residues. The procedure took hours – and then she scrubbed the pavement clean.

At least Tom and Jinnie had the pleasure of knowing that Lew *did* finally manage to go to college and train as a teacher. They loved his wife, Nancy, and her presence helped them to deal with the War years when Lew was serving abroad in the Royal Engineers. However, one of their greatest delights came when their little grand-daughter made her entrance into the world in 1944.

I loved Nana and Daddy Bom's house. There were two rooms upstairs and two rooms downstairs. The huge beds upstairs had mattresses that were so soft that I sank into them in the middle. There were always several layers of blankets with an eiderdown on top of them and a chamber-pot discreetly placed underneath. There was very little other furniture upstairs – a huge, dark wardrobe, an ottoman and a massive chest of drawers. There was a painting by Leonardo da Vinci called' The Last Supper' on one of the walls – and underneath the figures were the names of Jesus and all the disciples written in Latin. I spent hours trying to learn them by heart, fascinated by the 'U's that were written as 'V's.

Downstairs, there was the parlour that was only used for special occasions. Many meals were eaten in the kitchen but we sometimes had our evening meal in the parlour. The food always seemed to be the same – thinly-sliced bread with plenty of yellow butter on a special china plate, pickles and sauces, vegetables and cold meat. It was all accompanied by several cups of strong, sweet tea that kept hot in a brown teapot wrapped up in a cosy by the fire. Afterwards, there were pears that had been scooped out of a tin into a big, patterned glass bowl or a fruit tart made with apples or whinberries that we had picked from the mountain.

There was one strange feature of eating in the parlour. The meal usually coincided with the time of the doctor's evening surgery. This took place directly opposite our house and the table was near the window. Through the net curtains, we watched as the sick people waited outside in all weathers to be at the head of the queue. We watched as they filed inside and we could even see where they sat because their silhouettes were clear in the waiting-room window. We watched as they came out. Nana and Daddy Bom seemed to know everybody and all the grown-ups talked about how well or ill they looked; they noticed who came out with medicine or a piece of paper. Nana, in particular, was very good at guessing what these people's problems were. It was a strange kind of entertainment to accompany a meal.

It was in the kitchen that most things happened. The black kettle was permanently boiling on the coal fire. Tucked in neatly on both sides of the fire, there were two little black ovens that were always hot. I loved to watch Nana pop a pale whinberry pie in one of them and see it come out later, golden brown with the sizzling fruit juice seeping out of the knife-cut gaps in the pastry. It was very exciting if I had helped out earlier on! Sometimes, before it went into the oven, I was allowed to dip a fork in a little saucer of milk then press it onto the edge of the pie to make striped marks in the pastry. This bit on the edge came out browner than the rest and it was delicious to eat.

There was a big clock on the wall above the table and Nana sometimes let me climb up to wind it up. I had to stop the pendulum, bring out a huge key and turn it round in a little hole before putting it back in its place. Then, very gently, I started the pendulum again. This was an important job. Everybody sat down at six o'clock in the evenings when the wireless was turned on for the news. There were announcements to ask people on holiday to get in touch with their families because someone was dangerously ill in a hospital on the other side of the country. The grown-ups looked at each other anxiously. Then, another, louder clock than ours, chimed and a very serious-sounding man told us all about what had happened in the day. Sometimes, someone had died or was very ill or there was something going on in London. Six o'clock was a very sad time. Nana, Daddy Bom and my parents all sighed or looked shocked. I can't remember there being any 'good' news.

The little wooden table in the kitchen was the only big, flat surface. Whenever it was not being used for anything, it was covered with a chenille cloth. For washing-up or preparation of food, the cloth was folded away and the table was covered with newspapers placed on top of the bare wood. This was to protect the table so that it wouldn't get stained. When someone got washed, the newspaper was kept in place with a towel ready, warm from the fire. I used to watch my parents as they prepared to go out in the evenings with friends. First of all, my father had the clean, hot water. He washed, then lathered shaving foam all over the bottom half of his face with a brush before shaving it all off again! As he did so, he looked in the mirror to make sure that he didn't cut himself. Then he put Brilliantine on his lovely dark hair and changed into smart clothes. More water had been boiled in the meantime for my mother. She washed in the fresh water, cleaning her face with a flannel and then she began to put her make up on. There was the powder and the Bourjois rouge, patted on then smudged away so that it was hard to tell that it had been applied in the first place. Then, there were the eyes. She spat onto the block of mascara and pulled a little brush across it before putting it on her eyelashes to make them long and curly. Then there was the lipstick. She made a funny pout in the mirror and pressed the stick onto her lips to make them a dramatic red. Then she licked one lip against the other to set it and spread the colour evenly. She brushed her hair this way, then that way, so that she had the curls where she wanted and, finally, she sprayed on her perfume. 'Evening in Paris' in a blue and white box and 'Californian Poppy' in a red and white one, were her favourites. When she had changed her clothes, the two of them went out together – my father smart and handsome and my mother pretty and happy.

Being on my own with Nana and Daddy Bom in the evenings

suited me well. They let me stay up late and I had treats. I had already discovered the delicious toast with the salty Welsh butter!

One evening, Daddy Bom asked Nana if he could have a florin to go to The Bird in Hand. Nana said 'No' but Daddy Bom engaged in some flattery and persuasion – something he was very good at! He winked at me, Nana relented and he got his own way. When he came back from The Bird in Hand an hour or so later, Daddy Bom seemed very happy. Beaming at me, he put his arm round Nana and sang her a song:

> 'We've been together now for forty years,
> And it don't seem a day too much,
> There ain't a lady living in this land
> As I'd swap for my dear ole Dutch.'

I didn't understand the words at all but they made Nana laugh and it all seemed to be well worth a florin.

In the summer, Nana and Daddy Bom took me to Porthcawl for a week. We stayed in a guest-house run by a big, apron-wearing lady from Lancashire and her husband who smoked so much pipe tobacco that his fingers and moustache were stained a brownish-yellow colour. During the day, I played on the beach and I loved to walk up on the Esplanade when the tide was high so that I could run away from the splashes as the waves hit the rocks – straight into Daddy Bom's arms. There was a lot of laughter. We went to the fairground and Daddy Bom and I always shared a seat in the water-chute as Nana watched. As I held onto him tightly, the little car went up so slowly that I thought we might slide back, then the speed gathered pace as we turned a corner at the top before gliding down to be splashed by the water. We screamed with delight at the fun. The three of us went on a ride called Around the World where we got into a little boat that took us around a dark canal. At every corner, we met a different country. There was Holland with tulips and clogs and Dutch girls wearing those strange hats. Then there was India and more… For several years, I was convinced that I really had travelled round the world!

I went with Nana and Daddy Bom once on the bus to a hospital where they were seeing about the 'compo' money. I'll never forget the atmosphere in that room as men in their vests and long johns queued up for tests while their wives held the rest of their clothes. I could feel the anger in the air as the chance to have enough money to survive depended on the poor state of their sick husbands' lungs. Daddy Bom didn't have quite enough dust in his lungs at the time and, on the bus home, Nana and Daddy Bom did what they always did when I was with them. They laughed and joked. But I knew that they were only pretending and I wished that they could hear his cough.

Who makes decisions when doctors disagree? Maybe an observant child who has seen things at close hand is as shrewd as anyone. I would have stood up in any court, addressed any doctor – and told them about Daddy Bom's cough. I would have told them about the pain and the hardship. At the age of eleven, I was certain that an injustice had been done.

ENDNOTE

What became of the descendents of Harry and Jane Griffiths and Tom and Jinnie Williams as the twentieth century drew to a close?

Jinnie herself was over eighty when she died in 1975. After a stroke and with painful arthritis, she continued to be active, climbing ladders at perilous heights to wallpaper her ceilings. It was only in her last few years, after a pelvic fracture, that she deteriorated. Jinnie's longevity enabled her to see the significant success of Lew and Nancy's teaching careers. She was able to send me a telegram when I qualified as a teacher myself. She had the sadness of seeing me struggle for years with bi-polar affective disorder and temporal lobe epilepsy (probably caused by head injuries sustained when I was three years of age) and these were conditions which necessitated frequent hospital admissions. However, Nana also survived long enough to walk (with difficulty) to my wedding and her happiness was evident in the photographs. A year later, she was thrilled and excited to hold her great grand-daughter in her arms.

Peggy, Nancy, Owen and Nesta (the children of Henry and Jane Griffiths (née Lloyd)), were all very strong personalities and everyone thought that they would live forever. They all had a long life-span but they died within two years of each other.

Peggy died in December 2000. Confident, assertive, house-proud, beautiful, she was a typical first child. Her first husband, Phil, was a genteel Englishman who loved sport. He was related to the Compton family (Dennis, the cricketer and Leslie, the footballer) and Peggy found herself in the midst of a prestigious social circle. She had two children, and continued with the nursing career at which she excelled. Phil died suddenly in late middle-age and Peggy was devastated. She eventually re-married and used her retirement to focus on her grandchildren and work as a guide at Hatfield House. Her historical knowledge was photographic and many people said that her lively commentary made the place come alive for them. Though she seldom returned to Wales as an adult, her daughter chose a song for her funeral that began with the words 'I am dreaming of the mountains of my home...'

Two months later, in February, 2001, Owen died. Owen had married Olga – a charming, warm woman who loved him as a wife and friend. She did a lot of mothering – apart from her own three children, Olga was maternal with Owen. He trained as a teacher but left teaching to become a solicitor. Later in his life, he became a coroner and was eventually the Deputy Coroner for Birmingham. Owen was a strict disciplinarian and a perfectionist who expected the best from everybody. He didn't suffer fools gladly, but those who knew him best said that there was a soft heart inside. He was reduced to tears by the fact that he had no memory of his mother. His funeral included a hymn that he had translated himself from the Welsh and a commissioned stained-glass window in his memory was entitled *Y Bugail Da* (The Good Shepherd). It shows a shepherd holding a lamb. The ewe snuggling up to the shepherd was added to represent that early maternal loss.

In September 2002, Nesta died. Nesta had married a Cardiganshire farmer, Bill, and was the only one of Henry and Jane Griffiths' children to keep her Welsh and pass it on to the next generation. Bill was a quiet thinker and Nesta was a prolific talker. She was beautiful, a lively extrovert, an excellent cook, farmer's wife and businesswoman. The couple lived on Bill's farm in Tregaron for many years with their two children before moving up to live and work in the dairies that Bill owned in London. Apart from her business and her family, Nesta remained active in her chapel-life, continued to sing, write poetry and compose some hymns. I was privileged to be her confidente – especially towards the end of her life. Nesta suffered from a bi-polar affective disorder. When she was depressed, she wrote some of her most poignant poetry. When she was 'high', she was very funny. Bill and Nesta managed a shop in Aberystwyth as a 'semi-retirement' venture; it sold groceries, sweets, cigarettes and ice-cream. One St. David's Day, she put a sign on the shop window – '*Popeth yn rhad ac am ddim heddiw*' (Everything free today). When Bill saw it, he muttered '*Dim ffordd i rhedeg busnes yw hwn, Nesta fach.*' (That's no way to run a business, Nesta, love.')

Two months after Nesta's death, my mother, Nancy, died in November 2002. She had achieved many things in her life. She had been the Headmistress of an Infants' School in Essex, the Deputy Head Teacher of a larger Primary School and President or Member of countless organisations and committees. Parents always hoped that their children would be in her class because she was so effective. She retired with my father to Llandrindod Wells where she continued to have an active life for almost twenty years. A fun-loving, chatty extrovert, she worked for the Church (especially for the Leprosy Mission), the League of Friends in the local hospital, and Probus; and she loved dressing up and taking part in the town's Victorian Week. Pretty and fashionable, vulnerable yet tough, strong-minded yet soft-hearted, she endeared herself to many people. When a water-feature and plaque were installed in her memory at the local hospital almost a year after her death, most of her friends were still moist-eyed at her loss.

All the Griffiths' children died in that short period of time but they were not the only ones. In the midst of all these bereavements, my father, Lewis (Lew – the only son of Tom and Jinnie Williams), died in April 2001. He had always enjoyed good health but he was very ill for a few years at the end. Like Nancy, he had done well in his teaching career. At various times, he was Head of Mathematics and Religious Studies in Comprehensive Schools in Essex. He was also Head of the Sixth Form and the first Careers Master in that county. Handsome, proud, passionate, strong-willed, he was another disciplinarian at work. He had an active retirement too and was well-respected for his thoroughness in any venture that he undertook. Nothing that mattered to him was done half-heartedly. His early background had fostered cautiousness which was well-balanced by my mother's impulsiveness! They were well-travelled and enjoyed their holidays with relatives in the States; they had also visited most countries in Western Europe. Both he and my mother, Nancy, were devoted to their grand-daughter (my daughter), Meleri. They welcomed my husband, Peter, into the family as they did Huw, our son-in-law.

Most of the other close descendents of Tom and Jinnie Williams (née Lewis) also died within the space of those few years, taking away the bulk of an entire generation. Ray and Jenny (the two surviving daughters of William John Lewis) died in London; Gwendo and Margery (David Lewis' daughters), Doris (the daughter of Lewis John Williams), and Iris (Lew's closest lifelong family friend) all passed on.

My daughter married a fellow Welsh doctor in 1998 and I became a grandmother for the first time in 2002. My mother, Nancy, lived long enough to see, hold and marvel at her first great-grand-daughter. I was fortunate enough to have a second grand-daughter in 2005. My relatives are scattered all over the country now and people's lives have generally become busier. However, we share the same inheritance and I hope that this will be sufficient to make us want to keep in touch with each other.

These are my people, my kith and kin. I am grateful to each

one of them. I hope that, through writing about them, I have understood them better. I pray that those who have died may rest in everlasting peace and that, those of us who are alive or yet to come, will continue to be inspired by their courage and endurance.

Notes of Interest
on the Text

David and Anne Griffiths

The Church in Mathri is dedicated to the Holy Martyrs – these
are usually perceived as being the seven sons rescued by St.
Teilo. In and around the building are several significant historical
stones. The Church is on the Saints and Stones route. For more
information, see *Saints and Stones* (Gomer Press. Damian Walford
Davies/Anne Eastham)

Benjamin and Margaret Griffiths

Benjamin and Margaret lived initially at Bwchdu cottage. It still
stands on land owned by Peter George of Llanferran Farm. The
author visited it in 2006. It has been uninhabited since 1950 and,
apart from having a new slate roof, it is similar to the home that
Benjamin and Margaret would have known. There is a half-loft,
the original earth floor, *y simne fawr*; a lintel is made from wood
retrieved from a shipwreck. The original enclosed garden is there
– as are the ruins of the cowshed and the pig-sty.

Later in their marriage, the Griffiths family moved up to one
of the Castell cottages in Llanwnda. Two of the original four
cottages remain. Jack (Pontiago) Williams has the original records
of daily life on the Pencaer Peninsular and the author has seen
details of payment made to Benjamin and his family.

Thomas and Phoebe Jenkins

Thomas and Phoebe lived in Gwndwngwyn. The building is still
there, modernised and a sought-after 'cottage to let'! It is very
close to Pwllderi – the site that inspired Dewi Emrys to write his

famous poem of the same name.

To mark the 200th anniversary of the Last Invasion of Britain by the French at Carregwastad, local women made an impressive tapestry depicting the event. It measures 30.4 metres long, 53 cm deep and is on permanent display in Fishguard Town Hall. There is a stone to mark the site of the invasion at Carregwastad Point. Jemima Nicholas is buried in the churchyard of St. Mary's, Fishguard.

The Lloyd Family

The Lloyd family of Little Newcastle was well-known. Colston Farm is still there and so is the modernised cottage where Samuel and Mary Lloyd lived with their children. The two Neolithic burial chambers are located close to Colston.

St. Peter's in Little Newcastle is another Church on the Saints and Stones route. John Wesley, William Williams (Pantycelyn) and Howel Harries all preached here. The font dates back to the twelfth century and the Church is enhanced by stunning, contemporary stained-glass windows. These were designed by staff and students at the Swansea Institute, which has a noted Faculty in that medium.

The rhyme to welcome in the New Year in the text is still used in Little Newcastle. Until the beginning of the twentieth century, Little Newcastle joined in with the tradition in the Gwaun Valley (Pembrokeshire) of celebrating the New Year on January 12th.

There is a memorial in the village to Barti Ddu – the notorious pirate who hailed from Little Newcastle.

For more information on the other ancient monuments, settlements and wells in the area, see the book *Saints and Stones* (as mentioned above).

North Pembrokeshire

It's worth noting that a substantial part of North Pembrokeshire is richly endowed with standing stones, ancient settlements and burial chambers. There are many books and websites available detailing their history and locations.

Henry and Jane Griffiths

Accounts of the story of the Well in Abercynon and the pilgrims who subsequently flocked there in search of healing, were featured in the *Western Mail* during the 1920s. Although it has declined in popularity, visitors still come to the shrine from time to time. It can be reached by going into the grounds of St. Thomas' Roman Catholic Church and taking a pathway down towards the river on the left. St. Thomas' Church is usually open during the day for prayer.

Lewis and Elizabeth Lewis

For a while, Lewis and Elizabeth lived with their young family at Henry Square, Abercanaid. (see JOHN AND ANN WILLIAMS).

Lewis and Elizabeth's daughter, Ann, moved with her husband, John Williams, from Abercanaid to Cwmaman. The coal-mining days are over but Cwmaman has retained its close-knit sense of community. The Cwmaman Institute, which was so widely-used by the miners, has been given a new lease of life. Amongst other things, it now caters for wedding parties and is the base for film festivals with its superb Theatre and Cinema space (www. cwmamaninstitute.co.uk). A major figure in the spearheading of this enterprise has been Ian Roberts, who is the great-grandson of Lewis and Elizabeth Lewis.

John and Ann Williams

At the time of his marriage to Ann Lewis, John Williams lived at 72, Nightingale Street, Abercanaid. It was typical of the coal-miners' cottages at the time – one room downstairs and one room upstairs. It is now a Grade II listed building. Nightingale Street is close to the canal. For two generations, the family had the advantage of living in some of the most inspired buildings that were erected at the time for Industrial workers. Ann's parents had lived in Henry Square – one of three exceptionally well-constructed Squares in Abercanaid. The houses by the canal were also built to make living conditions as pleasant as possible. Lewis and Elizabeth went on to live right by the canal – as did John and Ann Williams when they first married.

At the end of his life, Rees (the son of John and Ann Williams), lived in Llanwonno Road, Cwmaman. The well-known writer, Alun Lewis, was born in the same street (a blue plaque on the exterior wall marks the house).

Morgan and Sarah Williams

Morgan and Sarah lived in the village of Llanarthne, which is now the site of the impressive National Botanical Gardens of Wales (www.gardenofwales.org.uk)

John and Sarah Lewis

There is a beautiful bronze statue of Caradog in Victoria Square, Aberdare by William Goscombe John.

BIBLIOGRAPHY

Life and Traditions in Rural Wales, W. J. Geraint Jenkins (Dent 1976)

Welsh Folk Customs, Trefor M. Owen (National Museum of Wales/Welsh Folk Museum 1968)

Tradition and Folk Life: A Welsh View, Iorweth C. Peate (Faber and Faber)

Welsh Folk-lore and Folk Custom, T. Gwynn Jones (Rowman and Littlefield)

The History of Wales, J. Graham Jones (Cardiff University of Wales Press/ *Western Mail* 1998)

Wales and Britain 1900-1951, Roger Turvey (Hodder and Stoughton 2002)

The Welsh Language Today, Ed. Meic Stephens (Gomer Press 1973)

Wales and the Welsh, Trevor Fishlock (Cassall and Co. Ltd 1972)

Merthyr, Rhondda and the Valleys, A. Trystan Edwards. (Robert Hale Ltd. 1958)

Working Iron in Merthyr Tydfil, Richard Hayman (Merthyr Tydfil Heritage Fund 1989)

Aberdare Urban District Handbook and Directory, 1960

Abercynon: Past and Present, compiled by Rowland Parry (Chalford Publishing Company 1996)

Fishguard and Goodwick, the Official Guide, third edition

Newport, Pembrokeshire and Fishguard, compiled by Martyn Lewis (Chalford 1996)

An Authentic Account of the Invasion by French Troops on Carregwastad Point in Fishguard, 1797 (Pembrokeshire County Council Cultural Services 1997)

St. Peter's Church, Little Newcastle. A Directory of the Churchyard, Richard Davies (Pembrokeshire Press, Fishguard 2000)

Teyrnas y Glo, Bill Jones, Beth Thomas (National Museum of Wales 1993)

Children in the Mines and *Aberdare from the Past* (Volumes 1 and 2) (Cynon Valley History Society 1987)

The Book of Welsh Saints, T. D. Breverton (Gwasg Y Bont 2000)

Chwedlau Gwerin Cymru, Robin Gwyndaf (Amgueddfa Genedlaethol Cymru 1992)

Saints and Stones, Damian Walford Davies and Anne Eastham (Gomer 2002)

Letterston Parish Council 1894-1994, Letterston Community Council (research Kathleen Evans)

Land of my Fathers, Gwynfor Evans (Y Lolfa, 7th impression 2005)

Real Wales – a Guide, Heini Gruffudd (Y Lolfa 2001)

Aberdare: Pictures from the Past (Cynon Valley History Society 1998)

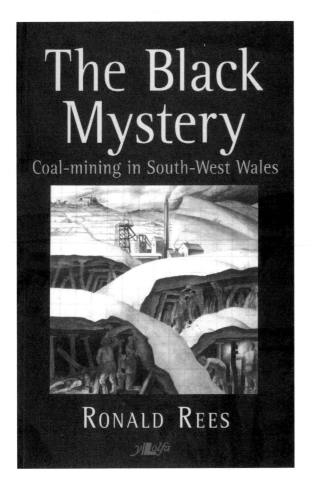

Am restr gyflawn o lyfrau'r Lolfa,
mynnwch gopi o'n catalog newydd, rhad
neu hwyliwch i mewn i'n gwefan·

www.ylolfa.com

Ile gallwch archebu llyfrau ar lein.

TALYBONT CEREDIGION CYMRU SY24 5HE
ebost ylolfa@ylolfa.com
gwefan www.ylolfa.com
ffôn 01970 832 304
ffacs 832 782